Praise for

90
Days
to **Live**

Alternative Cancer Treatments have been stymied for far too long by a myriad of regulatory, financial, and political issues blocking patients from getting the full spectrum of healthcare options available to them. This brave book is the compelling story of one couple who dared to go 'outside the box,' and after embarking on a remarkable journey, were able to beat the odds through a combination of sheer determination, persistence and hope as they integrated little-known approaches. A must-read for anyone feeling trapped by their choices and thinking there's no hope."

—Dr. Eric Wood, ND
www.drericwoodnd.com

"Rodney and his wife Paige take us on their challenging personal journey to discovering a more natural way to conquer Rodney's Non-Hodgkins Lymphoma. In the face of an alarming prognosis from the doctor (summed up in the book's title), this couple forged ahead in their decision to take an alternative route rather than go with traditional chemo and radiation treatments. Their story takes us through the day-to-day experience of holding onto hope as they change their lifestyle through nutrition and cleanses. An inspirational story for anyone facing a critical health condition. A hearty round of applause for this couple's perseverance, strength and bravery!"

—Cynthia Olsen Author
Essiac: A Native Herbal Cancer Remedy
Gold Medal Small Press Book Award
http://www.cynthiaolsenauthor.com

"*90 Days to Live* is the refreshing, encouraging, inspiring true story of an American couple Rodney and Paige Stamps. Rodney was diagnosed with Non-Hodgkin's Lymphoma, a deadly form of cancer. Without chemotherapy, the oncologist's prognosis for Rodney was 90 days left on this Earth. (Statistically, chemotherapy procedures yield a 2.1% cure rate, i.e. five years. Translation? Out of one hundred treated individuals, two will make it to five years, and 98 won't.)

In plain language, the book recounts Rodney and Paige's efforts to beat the odds by successfully avoiding the toxic route, and combatting cancer naturally. In vivid fashion, the book highlights the couple's determination to save Rodney's life through alternative methods that they disciplined themselves to follow. The book also tells the successful story of a *loving, understanding* joint venture. I recommend the book to anyone seeking a *natural and safe* approach to survival."

—Dr. E.K. Schandl

Director, American Metabolic Laboratories

https://www.americanmetaboliclaboratories.net

90
Days
to Live

90 Days to Live

Beating Cancer
When Modern Medicine
Offers No Hope

One Couple's Incredible *Alternative* Journey
to Curing the "Incurable"

Rodney
& Paige STAMPS

For information about this title or to order other books and/or electronic media, contact the publisher:

Verdavia Press, LLC
PO Box 31131
Edmond, OK 73003
info@verdavia.com

Library of Congress Control Number: 2018904921

ISBNs:
978-0-9993722-1-0 (print)
978-0-9993722-2-7 (ebook)
978-0-9993722-0-3 (audio book)

Printed in the United States of America

Cover and Interior design: 1106 Design

Names: Stamps, Rodney, author. | Stamps, Paige, author.
Title: 90 Days to live : beating cancer when modern medicine offers no hope, one couple's Incredible alternative journey to curing the "incurable" / Rodney and Paige Stamps.
Description: Edmond, OK: Verdavia Press, LLC, 2019.
Identifiers: ISBN 978-0-9993722-1-0 (pbk.) | 978-0-9993722-2-7 (ebook)
Subjects: LCSH Stamps, Rodney--Health. | Cancer--Patients--United States--Biography. | Healing. | BISAC HEALTH & FITNESS / Diseases / Cancer | HEALTH & FITNESS / Alternative Therapies Classification: LCC RC265.6 .S73 2019 | DDC 362.196/9940092--dc23

Disclaimer

We have tried to recreate events, locales and conversations from our memories of them. In order to maintain their anonymity in some instances we have changed the names of individuals and places. We may have changed some identifying characteristics and details such as physical properties, occupations and places of residence.

The authors are not health care providers or doctors and are not qualified to dispense medical advice. This book is for informational and educational purposes only! Much of the book is a statement of opinion in areas where the facts are controversial or do not exist. This book is not intended to prevent, diagnose, treat, or cure disease. This book is not a substitute for consultation with a physician. If you are seeking medical advice consult a licensed physician. The authors are not qualified to prescribe medical treatments or to recommend any form of health care. The reader should regularly consult a physician or other licensed health care practitioner in matters relating to his/her health and particularly with respect to any symptoms that may require diagnosis or medical attention.

Table of Contents

Foreword

NECESSITY IS THE MOTHER OF INVENTION. Out of necessity, Rodney and wife Paige, overcame his lymphoma cancer (for 13+ years now!) while simultaneously building a booming fire-safety business. It was their "Staying Power" (a term coined by UCLA basketball coach, John Wooden, the winningest coach in college basketball history) that carried them through some very dark days.

Rodney and Paige are part of the newer "wired" generation, who, while they respect professional advice, don't put it on a pedestal to the exclusion of all else.

With resourcefulness, commitment and discipline, they chose to proactively search the Internet for professional and lay information about Rodney's condition, and had the courage to buck conventional wisdom and follow their belief. They represent a trend I'm seeing more and more in my professional life.

Rituxan chemotherapy is a relatively successful conventional treatment for Lymphoma cancers, but Rodney chose a "road less taken"—one which required more courage, discipline and commitment than most human beings have. This was especially true when, after months of enzyme treatment, the cancer increased in size before its final decline.

I have known Pamela McDougle for all 35 years of my career as a urological and pelvic cancer surgeon. Pamela, a nutritionist, along with Nicholas Gonzales, an immunologist medical doctor, trained under Dr. William Donald Kelly, the original creator of the enzyme protocol Rodney used for treating his cancer.

Nick Gonzales trained under the famous Robert Good at Sloan Kettering (New York City) and showed that high-dose enzyme treatment could control pancreatic cancer growth. Meanwhile, with a modest practice in Boise, Idaho, Pamela has treated over 5000 patients with impressive success.

The program uses up to 70 capsules of enzymes daily between meals for at least eight months duration. Why so many? Because less than 10% of those ingested make their way into the bloodstream to affect the cancers. My professor at Harvard—Kurt Isselbacher in the department of Gastroenterology—demonstrated this effect many years ago studying the enzyme peroxidase.

The accepted scientific confirmation of the protease enzymes attaching to alpha Macroglobin and then affecting the Transforming Growth Factor thus allowing optimal host immune function may be an explanation for us professional researchers and medical doctors (J. Immunotherapy 21(2)85, 1998). One aspect well known, is that the Chymotrypsin protease is the most important enzyme for destruction of cancer growths as noted by Kelly, Gonzales and McDougle.

Enzyme therapy is just one part of McDougle's arsenal. Additionally, she not only attacks the cancer nutritionally—eliminating all sugar and refined carbohydrate intake—she also advocates for decreasing "body burdens" through colon cleansing with coffee enemas.

That's why Rodney lost thirty pounds (30+ lbs.) when he changed his diet. Today we know from PET scans that 90% of all cancers feed on sugars and carbohydrates. The scans show high sugar isotope uptake in breast cancers and Lymphoma. As such, avoiding these foods literally starves cancer cells to death.

After 35 years of managing cancer as a surgeon, my focus today is on how to use metabolic interventions in dealing with cancers with "abnormal fuel or energy systems." It's not my original work; credit goes to researchers like Otto Warburg, pioneer of cancer metabolism; along with my teachers, Albert Lehninger and Peter Pedersen of Johns Hopkins University Medical Center; and Tom Seyfried, author of Cancer As A Metabolic Disease.

Are cases like Rodney's lymphoma a fluke or just an anecdotal happening of chance? Definitely not! Thousands of people have benefitted from Pamela McDougle's work in Boise, and Nicholas Gonzales' clinic in New York City. During my years performing cancer surgery, and in conjunction with the National Cancer Institute in the *Best Case Series* under the leadership of Dr. Jeff White, I volunteered to audit institutions like Kushi and Hippocrates Institutes—which claim success with nutritional interventions for terminal cancer patients. To my surprise, we did see about one-third of the cases end up with impressive outcomes—a significantly higher success rate than that found with most conventional approaches.

To make further advances into formal clinical research is costly. As such, foundations like ours (YuFoundation.org) and others are working hard to raise enough money to make this happen.

It is not necessary, in order to make great progress in the cure of cancer, for us to have the full solution of all the problems of basic science research. . . . The history of medicine is replete with examples of the cures obtained years, decades and even centuries before the mechanism of the action was understood for these cures—Sidney Farber, the father of American Oncology, United States Congress 1971.

Why is this book so important? Because, as a reader, and possible cancer sufferer, you need to know that you CAN make a difference with your cancer. Nutritional and metabolic interventions are viable, and are forms of intervention that can be used alone or in conjunction with traditional treatments. Most importantly, there is plenty of good science behind these approaches.

Read this book. It will open your eyes to options you may be unaware of, and give you the power to actually do something about your cancer!

—George Yu, MD

Aegis Medical & Research Associates, YuFoundation.org, Clinical Professor of Urological Cancer Surgery, George Washington University Medical Center

CHAPTER 1

Out of the Blue

RODNEY

LIKE A BOLT OF LIGHTNING, Dr. A's words hit me. "I'm sorry, Mr. Stamps, but unless you start treatment immediately, about ninety days is all you can expect." I was alarmed and bewildered to think that my life could be over, when I wasn't even sick.

Rewind to six weeks earlier.

I woke up early, as usual, and it seemed like just another summer morning. I wasted no time because there were bridges to cross and mountains to climb and not enough hours in the day. How great to own my own business, call the shots, and let the buck stop here. Stampsco Fire and Security was taking off, and the future looked promising.

I hummed the melody to "Old Time Rock 'n' Roll" as I walked over to the closet. Traces of my distant past barely penetrated my present. I had given up that life as a drummer with a heavy metal band shortly after I met Paige, the love of my life. We were both smitten; I mean we fell hard. There was no question that we fit together like hand in glove, and, more than a decade later, our devotion was stronger than ever. Little did we know how that bond would be tested in the near future.

I carried my red shirt out of the bedroom, on my way to the kitchen. Pausing in front of the mirror in the dining room, I intended to put it on but stopped short. There was something above my left collarbone, something I hadn't noticed before. I moved closer, inspecting it with my fingertips.

It was a lump.

A large one.

I froze, with my arms suspended in midair before slowly lowering them. "Paige!" I realized I sounded more than a bit panicked, so I cleared my throat and reduced my volume a few decibels.

"Can you come here?"

She came running in. "What is it? What's wrong?"

"What do you make of this?" I asked, indicating the lump. "It's about the size of an almond."

"That's huge! How long has that been there?"

"No clue."

"How could you miss something like that?" she asked. Pausing a moment, she muttered, "How could *I* miss something like that?"

She stared at the bulge and told me I should go to the doctor again. Not my favorite thing to do. I had been to the walk-in clinic just a couple of weeks before; I was prescribed antibiotics and received a steroid shot for bronchitis, but a cough still lingered. Even so, I saw no need to go running back there, even if the lump was kind of scary looking.

I put on my shirt and headed to the garage to load up the truck, grabbing a chocolate-peanut-butter breakfast bar on the way out. Since the lump didn't hurt, I didn't worry too much about it. I figured it might go away if I just ignored it. No clinic for me that day. I was just too busy.

Several weeks went by, and life continued as normal. It was only when Paige and I were installing a fire alarm system at a high school with Tony, our lone employee, that I began to feel fatigued. The job required climbing up and down a few flights of stairs and oddly, I felt drained after just one climb. Come to think of it, I hadn't had much energy lately, maybe for several months.

"Looks like we need to invest in a treadmill," I told Paige, breathing hard as I closed my eyes against the stream of stars that fogged my vision. Maybe it was time to face the fact that I was pushing forty.

This day was like most others when you could find us, side by side, hard at work, blazing new trails and forging relationships with various clients to provide fire and life-safety systems.

Paige couldn't help but put in a little dig about all the cheeseburgers I ate and suggested that cutting back might be a good idea. My forehead was sweaty, my legs were rubbery, and Paige thought I needed medical attention. She thought I might be developing acute bronchitis.

I don't know why I resisted going to the doctor. I just didn't want to take the time. Paige thought it might be fear of the unknown or possibly had to do with the fact that they usually asked me to drop my drawers for a shot in the butt. Either way, it took some convincing to get me there.

I started to feel limp and wasted, so, within thirty minutes, I realized I needed to call it quits. I went out to our red truck and gave instructions to Tony, requesting that he wrap things up for the day.

Paige suggested that we go to the walk-in clinic where she had taken Jessika the previous week. Our fourteen-year-old daughter liked Dr. M. She had caught a bug and needed antibiotics. Since she'd recovered fairly quickly under his care, I nodded in agreement.

PAIGE

THE TRAFFIC WASN'T BAD ON THE WAY TO THE CLINIC. Rodney drove, and I rolled down the window, letting the cool breeze wash over my face, thinking about our family dog, a German Shepherd named Konan. His head would be hanging out the car window every chance he got. Though tempting, I didn't hang my tongue out, and I did my best not to bark incessantly at the people and dogs on the street.

When we pulled up to the clinic, the parking lot was fairly vacant, and hardly anybody was in the waiting room. They had tried to make the place as homey as they could, adding a few knickknacks here and there. Popular magazines lay on end tables with decorative lamps, and a few paintings hung meticulously on the almond-colored walls. I was glad that they hadn't chosen the bleak white color you normally see in medical facilities.

We signed Rodney in and awaited our turn on the cushioned chairs. I think it's accurate to say "our" turn, because I'm always there to see the doctor with my husband. If he went by himself, he might neglect to mention a symptom in order for the doctor to properly diagnose his ailment. Going to the doctor with a man is sort of like taking the dog to the vet. They seem to expect the doctor to make a diagnosis with little or no input from them.

When a nurse called us back, we stopped at the weighing station. I glared at the scale, thinking about how I never enjoyed standing on one. I would yank my shoes off, place my purse on the floor, and hope it didn't hit a new all-time high.

Rodney didn't seem to have any such qualms, though. Men. He plopped himself on the scale, boots and all, and watched the arrow hit 194 pounds.

He laughed and said, "Wow! I need to quit eating so much!"

I shook my head at him. "I'm sure those steel-toed boots you have on are adding a good eight pounds at least!"

No way would I have gotten up there with those boots on!

A few minutes later, Dr. M. came in. When he saw me, he gave a big smile.

"Hello, again! How's Jessika doing?"

"She's doing well," I said with a nod. "Pretty much fully recovered."

"That's good to hear," he said. "And you, Rodney? What brings you here?"

RODNEY

"I HAVE THIS LUMP above my collar bone."

Dr. M. raised his hands to my neck and felt around.

"That's an impressive lump. How long has it been there?"

"Not sure. I noticed it about two or three weeks ago."

Dr. M. continued to feel around, checking my neck, chest, and under my arms. Suddenly his hand stopped moving under my left armpit. "What's this?"

"What's what?" I asked.

"There's a huge lump in your armpit."

I heard Paige gasp as I quickly pushed his hand aside to feel the second lump. The thing was bigger than a golf ball!

How am I missing these things on my body?

Dr. M. began asking a barrage of questions.

"Have you had a fever?"

"No."

"Do you have a cough?"

"Yes. All I ever have is bronchitis. That's it."

I'm not the healthiest of specimens, but certainly not the sickliest, either.

I took a deep breath, trying to steady my nerves.

"Do you have any cats?"

Perplexed by his question I answered, "No. Why?"

"Your symptoms might line up with something called Cat Scratch Fever."

Great! A Doctor and a Ted Nugent fan!

"It's not uncommon for a person's lymph nodes to swell up from a cat scratch," he said.

"That would be a great answer, but we don't own a cat."

"Have you come across any cats lately?"

"No," I said, glancing over at Paige, who was pale and trembling. Turning back to the doctor, I asked, "What else do you think it could be?"

"I'm not sure." His calm exterior started to crumble, his eyes looking anywhere but at mine. "I'd like to run some tests to rule out certain scenarios."

"Okay," I said and then looked at Paige, who nodded.

He drew a blood sample and then walked out of the room.

PAIGE

STANDING UP, I WALKED OVER TO THE BLEAK TABLE where Rodney was sitting. Looking down at him, I kissed him on the forehead and rubbed the back of his neck. He was staring off into space and lost in thought; a deep furrow creased his forehead. I traced my finger across his brow and asked,

"What are you thinking about?"

"I don't know how I missed it. I take showers every day, and I've never felt it. Never! How could I miss something like this? It's not like it's smaller than the other one, either. It's huge! Feel it."

I lifted my hand up and felt it. He was right. It was huge, something he really should have detected earlier.

"I wonder what it could be?" he said.

The last thing I wanted to do was to share my worst fears with the love of my life, so I eluded the question.

One lump was startling, but two was terrifying. Entering the room, Dr. M. stated, "The lab is a little backed up, so I'll need to get back to you later this evening with the results of the blood test."

As Rodney and I walked out of the clinic hand in hand, I mumbled, "That's just great. I hate waiting! How long does it take to get blood results back?"

"I don't know."

I looked down at Rodney's hand entwined with mine.

I've always loved these hands.

Rodney would tell you that he's a leg person, but I'm definitely a hand person. You can tell a lot about a person by their hands, and my husband's hands are perfect. They were the first things I noticed about Rodney when we met.

Actually, the first time our paths crossed, I didn't even really see him. My friend, Sarah, and I were just hanging out in her cute little electric blue car with no real plans for the evening.

We howled along with a song playing on the radio, as we sped down the street, our long hair flying out the window, tangling in the wind. As soon as Sarah pulled into a gravel driveway, I pulled down the visor mirror to check out my makeup.

It was common for me to have lipstick streaks across my face after an exhilarating drive, because the wind would drag strands of hair across my lips, wisping them across my face.

Busy wiping my face, I briefly glanced over when Sarah's friend Johnny leaned down to talk to her through her window. I noticed someone with him, but all I could see were male legs, so I went back to touching up my makeup, vaguely wondering who he was.

Sarah finished her conversation, said goodbye, and threw the car into reverse. As she pulled out onto the quiet street, she looked at me and said, "He sure was cute!"

"Who?"

"Rodney. You know—the guy standing next to Johnny."

I shrugged. "All I saw were his jeans."

"Where do you want to go?"

"How about the pool hall?"

She rolled her eyes dramatically. "You know, you really should get a life."

"Just because I don't chase boys around like you do doesn't mean I don't have a life."

I was used to having this conversation with my friend. I'm not sure why I felt compelled to try to explain myself each time, because it never seemed to make a difference to her. She thought I was some recluse—a loner, I think.

Sarah finally shrugged her shoulders and sped to Pool Sharks, where I was a regular. She never minded the experience, because it gave her a chance to flirt with the boys, while I took their money. It was a symbiotic relationship.

A few days later, Sarah called me up.

"Rodney's playing the drums tonight. Want to go hear him?"

"I can't. I have something of a date tonight."

She laughed. "What's that mean?"

"A guy from the pool hall is going to teach me some shooting techniques."

"Sounds romantic."

"I did say, 'something of a date.'"

She shook her head. "Yeah, I'll give you that. So, when's this Casanova picking you up?"

"About seven."

She thought for a moment and then said, "How about I pick you up now, and you come with me until your date? I'll have you back before he arrives."

"I guess that will work."

Ten minutes later, she was standing on my doorstep. I opened the door dressed in a pair of holey jeans and a comfortable T-shirt. She was decked out to the hilt, with a cute blouse and miniskirt, her hair flowing around her shoulders.

"Wow, you look great!" I said.

"Thanks!"

We drove over to Rodney's house and knocked on the door. Johnny answered, inviting us to come in. Sarah and Johnny started talking, so I sat down on the brown sofa in the corner of the room.

As I waited for Sarah to finish her conversation, a guy with long, brown hair and forest-green eyes came out of the hallway. He was wearing black leather pants with a silver belt buckle, a black heavy metal T-shirt with the sleeves torn off, and black cowboy boots. I think I stopped breathing for a moment.

Hello, gorgeous!

He never even glanced my way, so I sat there and watched him get ready, kicking myself for having made plans with the other guy. I'd much rather watch this beauty play the drums. My eyes dropped to his hands. Tan, strong, and manly!

Oh, wow! He's one fine specimen!

A pothole in the road ripped me away from my daydream, hurtling me back to the present. I glanced over at Rodney, who was also lost in thought. Nearly home from the clinic, I looked around, wondering how the rest of the world could look so calm when my insides were churning like I was on some roller coaster that wouldn't end. My head and heart raced, in what could only be described as a panic attack.

I hate those things. They always strike at the most inopportune times.

As Rodney maneuvered through our neighborhood, I tried to give myself a pep talk. I didn't want anyone to guess what was going on inside my head, especially not Rodney. I had to stay calm and just get through it. By the time Rodney pulled into the driveway, I hoped I was prepared to face the world.

I saw our girls playing in the front yard. A friend had been watching them, and they looked so happy and carefree. Little did they know . . .

Just take a deep breath.

Rodney hopped out of the truck, and I slowly followed. Our girls are pretty bright, so they immediately looked concerned when they saw my face. Neither could read their dad's expressions, but I was an open book.

So much for my preparations.

They ran up, staring at us with their big, questioning eyes.

There was no way I was going to tell them anything until we knew for sure what was wrong. No sense in giving them the same scare I'd just experienced. Although I knew deep down that my beloved had cancer, I clung to any hope I could that I was wrong. It wasn't cancer until the last lab result confirmed it.

"I haven't been feeling well, so I went to the doctor," Rodney said. "Hey, Jessika, Dr. M. says, 'Hi!'"

"Oh, you saw him, too?"

"Yeah. He's a nice guy."

The girls ran off to play again, content that nothing could be too bad if their dad had just seen the same doctor as Jessika. After all, Jessika was back to normal, so he would soon be, too—right?

RODNEY

WHEN THE DOCTOR CALLED ME BACK THAT EVENING, he let me know that the blood tests were all normal. I turned to Paige and gave her a thumbs-up, which made her smile.

"That's awesome!" I said. I thought I had just dodged a bullet. I don't know why I had been so worried. I took pretty good care of myself. I was only in my late thirties and didn't smoke, drink, or abuse my body.

"I'm sorry, Mr. Stamps," Dr. M. said, pausing a beat. "I didn't mean to imply that you're out of the woods yet. I was just checking for a few of the basic illnesses, but the lumps still trouble me."

Dr. M. recommended that I follow up with a specialist as soon as possible to run more tests. When I asked what kind of specialist and he said, "oncologist," I was taken aback. It felt like someone had yanked my beating heart from my chest and handed it to me. My whole world was caving in on me.

Is difficulty breathing a symptom of cancer?

I muttered a thank-you and then hung up. Looking over at Paige, her stricken expression reminded me that I didn't have the luxury of self-pity. Her look indicated that she feared the worst.

I had to be strong for her. And if I were to have any hope of defeating whatever was growing in my system, I would have to stay positive.

"He says I should see an oncologist," I said, struggling to keep my voice from sounding as terrified as I felt.

It didn't work.

Paige immediately burst into tears. I pulled her into my arms and whispered soothing words, waiting for her sobs to cease and her body to finally relax against me.

"Sweetie, please look at me," I said.

Reluctantly, she complied, her eyes bloodshot, filled with more soon-to-be-shed tears. My heart went out to her, and I became even more resolved to beat whatever was wrong with me. I had a responsibility to my family to survive.

"I'm not going anywhere," I reassured her.

"You've always been my rock," she said, the color finally coming back into her cheeks. "If anyone can beat cancer, it's you."

"Hey," I said with a chuckle, "we don't know that I have cancer yet. Let's not jump the gun."

I felt so bad for putting her through what I feared was to come.

PAIGE

THE LAST THING I WANTED TO DO was leave Rodney's side, but I needed to check on dinner. Since nothing was on fire, I turned the heat to low, and we stepped outside on the back porch. We wrapped our arms around each other and were comforted, each by the presence of the other. The low light from the porch lamps spilled onto the concrete, saturating the night. Soon, moths fluttered in, encircling the ambient glow. They looked so peaceful and carefree as they danced around the blaze.

I wish I could stop time at this moment.

The girls were in their rooms, quietly reading and doing homework. I glanced inside and sighed. It suddenly hit me: *What are we going to tell the girls?* I had a sudden urge to run to them and give them each a hug. However, Jessika and Jade were both very astute and would immediately know that something was up. If they asked me a direct question, I'd be forced to tell them.

We decided to hold off telling the girls until we knew something more definitive. We hoped beyond hope that we never had to have that conversation.

I called the girls, asking them to set the table. Somehow, we managed to get through dinner.

Afterwards, I took a deep breath and then grabbed Rodney's hand, pulling him toward the living room. "Let's curl up on the sofa and watch something."

"How about a Disney movie with the kids?" he said with a sideways glance.

"Sure," I said. "Tonight you get to choose whatever you want."

Rodney threw in a movie, and I did my best to focus on the animated characters. I kept glancing over at him, trying not to be too obvious.

Are you as scared as I am?

I couldn't tell if he was or not, to be honest. He was good at hiding his emotions. Maybe some of his internal strength would rub off onto me.

I looked back at the television and tried to focus, but it was no use. My mind kept drifting back to our early years, to the moment I fell in love with him.

I was sitting at the house on a Saturday night, with Fleetwood Mac blaring from the stereo, waiting for a pizza to arrive, when the doorbell chimed.

I wasn't expecting anyone else that night, but, out of habit, I pressed my eye to the peephole to be sure there wasn't some masked murderer waiting on the other side of the door. I was a little surprised to see Sarah, and she wasn't alone.

I quickly opened the door. "Hey there! What brings you by?"

I looked past her, seeing Johnny, along with a few other people. One I knew, but the other man caused my breath to catch sharply. It was the gorgeous guy with the unforgettable hands. I could get lost in his twinkling eyes, but I found my gaze lingering on his lips. I couldn't seem to take my eyes off them.

I groaned internally when I suddenly realized I was sporting cut-off Levi's and a worn out T-shirt.

That's just great!

Sarah apologized for showing up unannounced.

Confusion caused her brow to wrinkle slightly. "What are you doing at home on a Saturday night by yourself?"

"I didn't feel like going out."

Sarah shrugged and motioned to the guy with the sensual lips and amazing hands. "Have you met the drummer from Johnny's band, Rodney?"

"No." I felt my face heat up, as I began to desperately wish that I had fixed myself up a little more before answering the door. Something I'd never bothered to do before.

"Rodney, this is Paige. Paige, Rodney."

"It's nice to meet you," I said, tilting my head in a way I hoped he'd think was cute, possibly even making up for my grungy clothes. I flashed him a smile for good measure.

He smiled back. "It's nice to meet you, too."

And just like that, I was smitten.

Since I'd ordered pizza, they all decided to stay and help me eat it. *Fine by me!*

I couldn't take my eyes off Rodney the entire time they were there. Unfortunately, he seemed to come with an attachment—Sarah's clingy sister, Stacy, who didn't seem interested in sharing.

Brokenhearted, I found a quiet corner of the living room where I could ponder my plight in peace, without having to watch Stacy hang all over Rodney. Here I'd found the love of my life, and he'd brought a date to my house!

My heart skipped a beat when he walked over to me, alone. I smiled broadly as he sat next to me on the love seat. We talked easily about various subjects, like pool and music. The chemistry was definitely there, and I could tell it wasn't just on my side. However, I didn't want to offend Sarah or Stacy, so I asked him if he was on a date that night.

"No," he said, looking over his shoulder. "Johnny just asked me to tag along and entertain his girlfriend's sister. It's really not a date or anything."

Good, because you're going to be mine.

It felt like we'd been friends for years, talking and laughing. I was having the time of my life when Stacy found us. She plopped herself onto Rodney's lap like a Pomeranian puppy and threw her arms around his neck. It took superhuman strength on my part not to reach out and smack her.

But when she put her slobbery lips on his, I lost it. I saw red and needed to put some distance between us. I stood up abruptly and said, "I think I'll leave you two alone!" before I walked out of the room.

I went into the kitchen to fume. It was hard to get away from them in my small home, but I did the best I could. A wave of loneliness threatened to engulf me as I stood alone in my kitchen.

How much longer will these people be here?

I turned around to get myself a glass of water when a breathless, disheveled Rodney came bursting into the room.

"There you are!" he said, looking greatly relieved. "Look, I'm not interested in her at all." He waved his hands in front of himself wildly, perhaps trying to erase the picture of their kiss from my mind.

It didn't work.

"Could have fooled me," I said, tapping my foot on the floor. I had intended the words to come out calm and cool, but I was too angry.

His lips formed a slight smile, and I melted.

Those lips.

He said something about trying to help his friend's girlfriend's sister, that there was nothing more to it, but I didn't know whether I bought it or not. I just nodded and left the kitchen.

Over the course of the evening, various male friends of Sarah came by, trying to entice me to go to the pool hall with them. Normally, I would've jumped at the chance to play, but I was too smitten with Rodney to even consider doing anything but staying home.

When I caught wind that Sarah was actually trying to get Rodney to leave, I shoo'd all the unwanted guests out. Rodney stayed another few hours, and we talked the entire time. He was and has always been a true gentleman. I was thrilled to find out later that he was equally attracted to me.

And now, this perfect man sitting next to me, watching a fairy tale with our two beautiful girls, might be ripped from my life in the most final way. I couldn't bear it. I snuggled even closer to him, laying my head on his shoulder and holding his hand as tightly as I could.

RODNEY

THE NEXT DAY, I WOKE UP FEELING HORRIBLE. I forced my body into a standing position and then pulled off my nightshirt, and Paige gasped. Alarmed, I went to the mirror and saw that my chest had swollen dramatically.

"I look like Arnold Schwarzenegger!" I said, flabbergasted. "But just on the left. I'm still Rodney on the right side."

My attempt at levity didn't have the desired effect. Paige glared at me. "Not funny! You're going to the ER right now!"

Smart enough to recognize that my sweet little wife had just given me a direct order, I knew better than to argue.

"I'm sure any doctor would know what to do," I said. "They've probably seen this before."

"What are you talking about? This isn't a sore throat or a light cough. Your left side is twice the size of the right! Maybe something's wrong with your heart? I'm taking you to the hospital right now."

We called a family friend to come watch the girls. As Paige drove me to the hospital, I could see that she was valiantly trying to stifle her sobs, but tears still streamed down her face, her body convulsing periodically.

"It'll be okay," I said, reaching over to pat her shoulder. "Just calm down. We'll get to the hospital, and everything will be fine."

She nodded and increased her speed. When we got to the ER, we had to wait about an hour to see a doctor. Paige and I tried to focus on the magazines strewn around the waiting room, choosing to put off the discussion of my health until a doctor could look at me.

Finally, we were escorted to one examination table among many in a large room. The nurse pulled a curtain around the small area to give us some semblance of privacy. Then we waited another twenty minutes for her to return to draw blood and take my vital signs. She wrapped up by telling us that the doctor would be in to see us shortly.

When he arrived, I did a double take. He was a dead ringer for the lead singer of the heavy metal band System of a Down. I looked over at Paige, and she was struggling to keep her shock from showing.

It's not just me, then.

The ER doctor was heavy set, with an unkempt beard, which looked like a wad of rusted steel wool had been glued to his chin. If that wasn't bad enough, he had huge, bulging eyes that made him look terminally surprised. What he didn't look like was someone with a degree in medicine. It only got worse when he started talking. His eyes bulged out even farther, while his fingers fidgeted with his white coat.

"The tests are inconclusive, but these symptoms are definitely indicative of something serious."

As he continued to speak, his face paled noticeably and mirrored the way I felt—frantic and terrified. I always imagined that doctors took a special course to train them on how to deliver horrible news to patients, learning to keep perfect composure. This doctor must have missed class that day.

I must admit, though, I could barely understand his words, because I was too absorbed in his facial expression. It seemed like he was trying his best to stay somewhat vague and objective but failing miserably. He obviously thought I had cancer.

Maybe I'd been dropped in an episode of *The Twilight Zone*, starring a far-out singer who was acting the role of doctor in this bizarre scene. Wouldn't it be great if I could just wake up?

Finally, Dr. Heavy Metal crumbled right before our eyes, completely derailed, and left the room, mumbling something about sending in another doctor to see us shortly.

Paige and I looked at each other, utterly baffled. Were we living in a twisted version of reality, or had that really just happened? It wasn't long before a more-traditional-looking doctor, a seasoned medical professional, walked in. No doubt, he'd been asked to try to salvage the botched conversation.

Although one might think that having an old pro take over where the foreboding, freaky doctor had left off might help ease the impact of the blow, it didn't. Once I saw how smoothly the new doctor went through his spiel, I realized the hospital staff had sent in their best, which meant there was something seriously wrong. You don't hire Michelangelo to paint a living room, and you don't send in a top-notch doctor to break the news that someone has tonsillitis.

I wish Dr. Heavy Metal would come back, tripping his way through his terrifying sentences and blinking his huge eyes way too much.

The seasoned doctor seconded Dr. M.'s assessment that I shouldn't have swollen lymph nodes and that I needed to see a specialist immediately.

When we got home, we tried to behave as normally as possible. For Paige, it was too much. Though she did her best to control her emotions, the lack of sleep and being super-charged on adrenaline made it impossible. Unfortunately, she ran out of the room crying at least three times during the course of the evening.

Our girls were perplexed at this uncharacteristic behavior, so I explained to them that Mom wasn't feeling well, combined with a poor night's rest.

The next day, I called the oncologist's office but couldn't get through. I figured they were just busy, so I left a message. Paige didn't approve of playing the waiting game, went straight to the phone, and called them herself. Getting the same recorded greeting that I had, she hung up, went into the kitchen, cleaned a few dishes, and tried again.

"You're going to see a specialist if I have to drive down there and pencil you in for an appointment myself!" she muttered as she hung up for the third time.

After about thirty minutes, she finally got through to the receptionist. I marveled at Paige's ability to get any task done.

That's my wife!

After she hung up, she smiled. "We have an appointment at two o'clock."

"Today?" I asked in disbelief.

"Of course."

I suppressed a grin.

"Wow. Nice work, Sweetie."

◆ ◆ ◆

The waiting room was filled with a variety of people. Some had full heads of hair, some didn't. Some were thin and frail, and most had a pale complexion. When we walked in, many heads turned to size us up. I felt a bit like a green-skinned alien with purple polka dots.

We were definitely the youngest and healthiest-looking people there, for now. They probably wondered which one of us was going to see the oncologist. Their unspoken question was answered when I approached the receptionist's counter.

Paige sat toward the back of the waiting room while I got my blood work done. Afterward, she admired the fluorescent pink wrap around my arm. I plunked myself down next to her and waited.

Not having much else to say, we just sat in silence, holding hands. It wasn't long before a nurse with red hair, freckles, and pale skin peeked her head out of the door and called, "Rodney Stamps!"

When we stood up and walked toward the open door, I noticed the nurse was a good eight inches shorter than Paige. Despite her short stature, she held herself with a quiet confidence. Flashing us a bright smile, I couldn't help but wonder, *How does she do that, when all she sees is cancer patients all day?*

After we walked through the door, I glanced to the left, down a narrow hallway, where patients sat in lounge chairs with IV bags dripping slowly into their arms.

That's probably where they administer the chemo.

"This way," the nurse said, heading down the hallway to the right.

She placed us in a freezing-cold white room that had a few well-read magazines thrown on a small table. Talk about sterile. The room was horrible. I climbed up onto the crinkly paper, feeling like a piece of meat ready to be wrapped and have a sticker slapped on stating how much I weighed and the cost. I looked around, half expecting to see white fitted jackets with the sleeves that strap around the back.

When we met Dr. A., Paige and I both liked him immediately. He was a tall man with a friendly face. I felt at ease with him. His questions were very familiar, so much so that I began to wonder if I should just carry transcripts from previous doctors' visits to hand to the current one. However, after we discussed the basic symptoms, the conversation diverged quite a bit from the norm.

"It sounds like Hodgkin's Lymphoma," Dr. A. said.

My heart sank. I was very familiar with Hodgkin's Lymphoma. An old business associate of mine had been diagnosed with that form of cancer when he was a young boy.

He had confided in me how, during his rounds of chemo and radiation in the hospital, he would befriend his roommates, other children who also had cancer. Sometimes he'd come back to his room after a treatment and find the neighboring bed empty and freshly made. When he would ask the nurse where his friend was, she would reply that the child had gone home.

When this happened again and again, he said that he finally figured out what was going on. His friends weren't going home— they were all dying. It was a tough dose of reality for any child to face.

From that moment on, he considered himself to be one of the lucky ones, because he had survived. Unfortunately, he died at age fifty-five from heart failure. When he passed, I wondered if the chemo and radiation treatment had something to do with his untimely death. All those chemicals and treatments are tough on the heart.

Doctor A.'s voice cut through my memories. "Hodgkin's Lymphoma is a cancer of the lymphatic system. It spreads from one lymph node to another and is often isolated in the neck area."

For twenty-four hours, I had been nurturing the hope that I didn't actually have cancer but rather some other, more easily treated disease. However, that dream was being crushed with each passing moment.

Surely he's talking about someone else.

"What's the treatment?" Paige asked.

"I'd rather wait to discuss the particulars of treatment until we know more," Dr. A. said gently. "We won't know what we're looking at until we get a biopsy. First, though we need to schedule a CT Scan, so I can see which lymph node would be best to remove."

I nodded. "When?"

"I'd like to schedule it for tomorrow, if that's okay."

"Tomorrow's fine," Paige said before I could answer.

PAIGE

As Rodney went to handle some paperwork, I leaned back in a chair in the waiting room and allowed my mind to drift back to our first date.

I was so excited to actually be going out with Rodney. When he'd asked me if I might like to see a few local bands play, I was a little hesitant. I quickly overcame my fears, though, because I knew this man was worth it. However, I worried that he'd mesh with this crowd while I stood out like a black duck on a lake of swans.

Rodney arrived on my doorstep wearing a T-shirt and holey jeans. I'd carefully chosen a black skirt with a black fitted blouse with gold buttons. I wanted to look my best.

The moment we set foot inside the club, I cringed. It was a seedy bar, complete with women trolling for any male who would look their way. A few of them even hit on Rodney right in front of me. Talk about a lack of manners!

Paige, we are in a bar. Did you really expect anything different? I asked myself.

Yes! Yes, I did!

As we walked over to a table in the middle of the room, where his friends were seated, Rodney seemed to sense my discomfort. He gave me a reassuring smile and gently slid his hand into mine, intertwining our fingers. When we reached the table, he pulled out my chair and scooted his next to me, sat down, and draped his arm protectively around the back of my chair. I felt laser beams from at least three other women, boring holes into my head from all angles.

Eat your hearts out, ladies!

I leaned back into the chair and listened to the band play songs from the eighties. They weren't bad. I was finally relaxing a bit when the lead singer suddenly called out to Rodney to come up and play with the band.

Rodney leaned toward me and whispered, "Do you mind if I go up and play a set with them? I won't be long."

I nodded, unable to think of a reason to say, "No." Honestly, I was torn. I'd miss his warm, comforting arm, but I was dying to hear him play.

Rodney looked over at his friend to the right. "Watch out for her while I'm up there. Okay, Squatty?"

"Sure, man," he replied.

No one could have picked a better nickname for the guy. Although it was rather unflattering, it was completely justified, seeing that he was about five-foot-five inches tall. He was a very sweet guy, with long, black hair and beautiful, crystal-blue eyes.

Rodney sauntered up to the stage like he owned it, taking the seat behind the drums. The minute the music started, he wreaked havoc on the set. Rodney fit right in with the screaming guitar and thumping bass.

He twirled the sticks, popping them up in the air off the snare drum and catching them on the way down, all the while keeping time with the band. Not that any recording studio would hire me to scout talent, but he was the best I'd ever seen.

Even though Squatty was put in charge of watching over me, he left to get a drink in the middle of the set. My body stiffened, and I counted the minutes for him to return.

At the table next to me sat a man with glazed eyes. He had noticed that I had lost my protection and decided to take advantage of the situation. He leaned his chair back on two legs and tried to put his head on my lap.

The first time, I managed to dodge the unwelcome gesture, but being determined, he tried again. Fortunately, Rodney had just finished up on stage and was en route back to our table when he caught a glimpse of the man's game. Rodney quietly sat down behind the unlikely suitor. When the man leaned back again, Rodney leaned over him and said, "What are you doing?"

It startled the man so much, he lost his balance, and his chair crashed to the floor!

As the man jumped up, ready for a fight, he said, "What's your problem?"

"You're disrespecting my girlfriend and me," Rodney said sternly.

The bouncer at the club came over and stepped between the two.

"What's going on here?"

The man was silent and staggered off to another part of the bar. Then, my knight in shining armor, dressed in jeans and cowboy boots, looked down at me and asked, "You ready to go?"

"Oh, yes," I replied, exhaling a sigh of relief.

As he drove me home that night, I couldn't keep my eyes off him. This wonderful man had stood up for me, something no one had ever done before. Despite having just met me, he protected me as if I were family.

When he pulled into my driveway, he walked around the car to open my door. Then he escorted me to my porch and asked, "Can I call you tomorrow?"

"Sure!" I probably sounded like a love-sick teenager.

"Maybe we can shoot some pool or something."

"That would be great," I replied, restraining my urge to clap with glee. "I love pool!"

"I know," he said with a chuckle. "Just go easy on me, okay?"

I nodded. Then he wrapped his arms around my waist and gave me a sweet, tender kiss goodnight before he returned to his car.

A perfect gentleman! Such a rare breed.

Reluctantly, I opened my eyes to the present, wishing I could stay in the past just a few more moments, but my chivalrous knight brought me back.

RODNEY

"YOU READY TO GO, SWEETIE?"

"More than you know."

Paige leaned against me as we walked out of Dr. A.'s office, her cheek on my shoulder. Her body was limp, trembling under my arm, and I could feel a growing wet spot on my shirt.

"Do you want to sit for a bit?" I asked.

"I just want to get home," she whispered between silent sobs.

"Let's go." She sounded exhausted.

I kissed the top of her head. "We'll get through this. I know we will."

She looked up at me, so forlorn and beaten. Her gut-wrenching moans cut me to the bone as I realized that she was affected as deeply as I was.

"How, Rodney? How on earth are we going to get through this one?"

I looked her straight in the eye. "I'm Superman."

She laughed. I could see her regaining a bit of strength as she nodded.

"You'll always be my Superman."

"That's my girl."

She wrapped her arms around my chest, squeezing me. "Hey, maybe you just have a few overzealous lymph nodes."

◆ ◆ ◆

The next day, Paige drove me in to have the CT scan. After I was checked in, I drank a large concoction of iodine that tasted horrid. It took all my willpower to keep the stuff down.

Paige requested to be with me during the scan, but the nurse shook her head. "Too much radiation."

The scan didn't take long. After it was complete, they put me in a room to wait for the radiologist to go over my results.

Before long, Paige came in. "How did it go?" she asked.

"It was pretty simple."

She paced the small room. "I just feel so helpless."

When she passed by, I pulled her to me. "I know."

A few moments later, the radiologist came into the room. "I just finished looking over your scan," he said.

"What do you think?" I asked, feeling my throat constrict as the words tumbled out of my mouth.

"Well, to be honest, I've never seen scans like this that weren't cancer, but we'll need to wait for the biopsy to confirm what's really going on."

Dead silence.

I caught my breath.

Although I appreciated his honesty, that was hard to hear. A bitter pill to swallow. Where's the spoonful of sugar to make those dreaded words go down easier? Here I was, in the prime of my life, with a beautiful family who needed me and my business just taking off. I needed cancer—*Not!*

Any remnant of hope that I didn't really have cancer had been extinguished by the radiologist's words. They kept repeating over and over in my mind, like a bad commercial.

I felt lousy and wasn't in the mood to talk to anyone that evening. Since we hadn't told our daughters what was going on, I had to maintain a cheerful façade, when really all I wanted to do was crawl into bed and sleep the next few days away.

No one felt like cooking, so we went out to our favorite Mexican restaurant for dinner. Normally, I'd scarf down my favorite, a Durango

Burrito, but that night, I could barely eat anything. My stomach kept threatening to spill its contents.

When we got home, Paige and I went to bed early and tried to sleep. But it was hard with the radiologist's words still haunting me.

I've never seen scans like this that weren't cancer.

They continued to echo through my mind. Surely there's been an error. How can I get my brain to calm down and sleep with a guillotine hanging over me?

Well, I'd just have to suck it up and wait. The biopsy was only a day away, and it would give us a wealth of information and a plan for how to move forward. A black cloud hung over us both.

The wait was interminable.

CHAPTER 2

Doom and Gloom

RODNEY

THE NEXT DAY, WE ASKED A FAMILY FRIEND to stay with the girls again, while Paige drove me to the hospital. We didn't say much to each other, each of us lost in our own thoughts.

When we arrived, they whisked me away and prepped me for surgery. I tried not to think about what was ahead of me and just got into the gown. When the nurse gave me stockings to wear, I looked at them in confusion.

"What are these for?"

"They'll prevent blood clots from forming in your legs during surgery," she said.

Great. A gown and panty hose!

Paige came in soon after, looking pale and fragile. "What's that?" she asked the nurse, pointing at my left arm. They'd drawn a purple circle around it.

"It's to tell the surgeon from which side to remove the lymph node."

"Wouldn't want to get that wrong, now, would we?" Paige muttered under her breath.

"Don't worry," I said. "It's all very routine."

Two single teardrops ran down her cheeks. "Might as well be brain surgery."

The anesthesiologist and doctor arrived together before the surgery. Their calm expression put me at ease, but Paige was still agitated. The surgeon gave her a sympathetic look. "It'll be a piece of cake." She nodded, and two more tears fell.

"It's time," the nurse said to her gently. "You can go out into the waiting room, and Dr. W. will update you once the surgery is complete."

Paige leaned over and planted a brief kiss on my lips. "I love you."

"I love you, too."

She walked to the door and then turned back to look at me. I could tell it was hard for her to leave me there, so I gave her a small smile, waved goodbye, and watched the door close behind her.

The nurse put an IV into my arm and raised the rails of my bed, before wheeling me down a long white hallway.

Is this how inmates on death row feel?

It suddenly hit me that I would be going under the knife within just a few minutes, that someone would be cutting my body open like a piece of meat. When I looked around, the medical staff seemed calm, like they'd gone through this hundreds of times, which helped me relax a little.

When we arrived at the operating room, the air was freezing, so they covered me up with several warm blankets. Everyone was wearing a green surgical mask, so all I could see were their eyes.

Behind me, the anesthesiologist said, "How do you feel?"

My eyes darted around the room, taking in all the machines and people. I wondered how long it would take for the drugs to kick in, for everything to go dark.

"Fine, under the circumstances."

He waited a moment and then asked, "How about now? How do you feel?" As he asked me that, my head started to feel funny, and I realized I wouldn't be awake for much longer.

"See you on the other side," I murmured. My eyes closed, and I heard the sound of low chuckles just before the room spun completely out of control.

PAIGE

WHILE RODNEY WAS HAVING A LYMPH NODE REMOVED for dissection, I closed my eyes, exhausted, hoping to grab forty winks, to no avail. My mind flitted back to a different time I'd had to sit in a waiting room.

Rodney and I had been dating for a few months, and I'd caught some kind of bug that wouldn't go away on its own. It was one of the rare times I'd visited a doctor.

Rodney offered to pick me up, because my car was on the fritz. I opted to wait for him inside the air-conditioned clinic, so I could avoid the sweltering July heat. As soon as he got there, I ran out the door and jumped into his car.

"So, did they figure out what's wrong with you?" he asked.

I shrugged. "They think I may be anemic."

"We just need to feed you more red meat, then!"

That was Rodney's answer to everything. Red meat. How did he eat so much of that stuff! The man was definitely a carnivore. Laughing out loud, I imagined him at a fine restaurant with a white linen napkin tied around his neck, a dinner fork in his left hand, a steak knife in his right, and, on a plate in front of him, a ginormous ol' filet.

Nearly fifteen years later, as I waited for the biopsy to be over, I was fighting back my fear of losing him. My whole life revolved around him in every way.

It felt like a month passed before the surgeon finally came out and said I could go see my husband.

RODNEY

WHEN I OPENED MY EYES A MOMENT LATER, I was in the recovery room. Paige was holding my hand, smiling at me.

"What happened? Is the surgery over already?" I asked.

"You did good," she said.

"Did you see my fancy socks? Let's not call them 'panty hose,' okay?"

She gave me a confused look but nodded at my socks. "They're great," she said unenthusiastically.

I looked over at the doctor. "So, Doc, what's the verdict? Is it cancer?"

He gave me a grim look. "We have to wait for the results of the biopsy from the pathologist before we can give you a diagnosis. Dr. A. will call you on Monday."

Monday? That's three days away!

When we got home, I went straight to bed. Before I fell asleep, Paige came in to change my bandage. Jessika made the mistake of walking into the room right as Paige was swapping the bloodied bandage for a fresh one and fainted dead away.

Paige scooped her up and carried her to her bedroom. "She's always been a lightweight when it comes to blood," she said when she returned. "She can't even pull turkey meat off the bone without getting queasy."

I nodded and felt my eyelids droop. With all the drugs in my system, I fell asleep quickly.

The next morning, I was sitting on the sofa in my shorts, experiencing the sweats like I never had before. My legs were actually steaming, like two freshly baked potatoes. My entire body was dripping like crazy, drenching towel after towel. Paige would try to put buckets under my legs to catch the drip, with little success.

That night was even worse. I woke up four or five times lying in a pool of sweat. Paige had to get up and help me change the sheets about every two hours. She did everything she could to set up my side of the bed with towels, but it didn't do much good. Neither of us got much sleep that night. That went on for days.

After the biopsy, the number of lumps exploded exponentially, spreading and popping up everywhere on my torso. Waiting for Monday to roll around was murder. Our lives hung in the balance as we anticipated the confirmation of my condition.

Things were beginning to take off at work, and the future looked promising. We were just hitting our stride. Only two years in business, and we were already in the black. We were so thrilled with our new company and had every reason to believe that it would grow rapidly if we continued working as hard as we had been.

Although I knew logically that it could only be the dreaded "Big C," I refused to give up until the doctor had officially diagnosed it.

Finally, Monday morning arrived. Paige and I hovered around the phone, willing it to ring and stop the agony of suspense. The anxiety was so great that my ears were hypersensitive to any sound. I must have jumped at least a dozen times, thinking every little noise was the phone. The anticipation was almost too much to bear.

When will this nightmare be over? Can't I wake up and have it all go away?

The girls were home, too, but didn't seem to have a clue about what was going on. We kept Jade home from school that day, and she didn't seem to question it. They occupied themselves happily outside. Jade drew chalk pictures on the driveway while Jessika practiced shooting hoops.

Every second that ticked by was pure torture. I was exhausted from pacing all morning and had little to no expectation that the oncologist would have any good news, but that didn't stop the surge of unrealistic hope from bubbling up inside me. I'll admit that I shamelessly clung to those last shreds of hope with everything I had.

When the phone finally rang, Paige stared at me with wide eyes. On about the third ring, I answered it and sat down on the couch.

"Hello?" *Man, my voice is trembling.*

"Is this Mr. Stamps?"

"Yes."

"It's Dr. A., calling about your biopsy."

I think my face had turned a nice shade of blue from holding my breath all weekend.

"Hey, Doc," I said as casually as I could manage. "Paige and I are eager to hear the news."

He paused for a minute and then said, "Do you want the good news or the bad news first?"

It's an age-old question that really has no correct answer. Any good news seems to always be wiped out by the bad.

Come on, Doc. Just rip the band-aid off, already.

"Let's go for the bad news first."

"It's definitely cancer."

I exhaled. "I agree—that's bad news," I said, slumping back into the cushion of the couch. I could tell that Paige had been able to hear that bit, because the color instantly drained from her face. She leaned back and closed her eyes.

"However, it isn't the type I was expecting," Dr. A. continued, almost as though I hadn't said anything.

So, is this the good news then?

"What type is it?"

"It's Non-Hodgkin's Lymphoma. As you know, lymphoma is a cancer that originates in the lymphatic system, attacking your immune system."

"So, what's the difference between Non-Hodgkin's Lymphoma and Hodgkin's Lymphoma?" I asked, still waiting to hear the explanation of why this could be deemed "good news."

"You can tell the difference between the two only by looking through a microscope, and another difference is in the treatment plans. Although Non-Hodgkin's Lymphoma has a worse prognosis, the good news is that it can be treated," he said.

"Great!" I said, breathing a sigh of relief. That is good news. "So, there's a cure."

"I didn't say that," he said. "There's a treatment. There's currently no cure for cancer, any kind of cancer." He paused. "Look, we need to schedule a time for you to come in and discuss the options in detail. I can't do them justice over the phone."

I closed my eyes. "When would you like to see me?"

"How's tomorrow morning at ten?"

I thought for a moment before saying, "Sure."

I must have sounded pretty dejected, because he said, "Listen, everything's going to be okay. Just come in tomorrow, and we'll put together a plan for you."

"Okay. Thanks, Doc," I said and hung up.

The moment I put down the receiver, Paige fell into my arms and cried. I couldn't think of anything comforting to say, anything that sounded real, so I just remained silent and held her tight.

As I held her, I realized that I was pretty ticked off. I suppose everyone responds differently to news like this. For me, it was anger. I think if the doctor had been in the room with me, I'd have wanted to clock him, even though he'd done nothing to deserve it. The messengers of bad news never have it easy.

It's fight or flight, Rodney!

If flight implies surrender, I vowed to stand up and fight. Surrender was not an option, and somehow chemo felt like surrender. It certainly was no victory if a cure was impossible and quality of life was shot to pieces. I wasn't ready to order a cemetery plot yet. No, that just wasn't me. My family needed me to stay alive.

I vowed at that moment to get any last trace of the cancer out of my body, completely. *This cancer will not win.*

After a little while, we walked into the kitchen, talking about what Dr. A. had said and discussing my possible options. No longer hungry, I just picked at the sandwiches that Paige had made earlier, which were lying on the counter.

I glanced out the kitchen window at my girls. They were playing in the front yard, laughing and running around, free from the worry of any problems that might exist in the world. That's the way it should be. They were young, vibrant, and full of life, and watching them gave me a short reprieve from the dreaded situation that loomed before me.

Now that all my worst fears had been confirmed, I had to find a way to tell them. But how do you tell your children that they might not have a father next year? I reeled when I realized the loss they might have to endure.

I have to convince them that I will beat this somehow, despite what the doctors say.

"What are we going to tell Jessika and Jade?" Paige whispered.

"We need to be honest with them, but I plan to let them know that I have every intention of surviving this."

Paige nodded but remained silent, her expression dejected. The worry and loss of sleep were taking a toll on her. Her nerves were obviously on edge. I had to change that. I had to give her hope, too. Research would help. I needed to understand this illness better, interview people who were living with it, learn what others did when faced with the same prognosis. What works? What doesn't?

I already knew chemo was iffy. I had two relatives, close relatives, who died from the stuff. Not much of a recommendation. I couldn't see going that route, but I was determined to keep an open mind. I'd take a scientific approach and not rule anything out until I'd checked it out thoroughly.

My attention turned to my friend, who was talking to Paige about various options. I listened, but no one seemed to have anything new to say.

"Do you know anyone with cancer?" I asked Paige.

"Just the same people you know," she replied.

"Anyone still alive?"

She shook her head. "No."

A hush fell over us. It might not be that easy to find cancer survivors, but I would scout them out. I needed to find people who had beaten the unbeatable disease.

Suddenly, Linda, a friend who had been watching our daughters in the front yard, rushed in, her face pale.

"I'm so sorry. I told them."

What are you talking about? "Told who what?" I asked.

"I told the girls you had cancer! I can't tell you how sorry I am. The words just tumbled out of my mouth before I could stop them."

Behind her, Jessika and Jade came trailing into the house. Jessika looked faint, while Jade was crying torrents of tears. They looked up at me, their sweet faces filled with questions and confusion.

This isn't how I wanted to do this!

"Come on into the living room, girls," I said, keeping my voice as calm and confident as I could. "I'll answer all your questions."

Linda came over to me as I was walking behind my daughters. "I'm so sorry," she whispered. "I just didn't know what to say, so I went for the truth."

You could have tried, "Ask your father."

I knew Linda was just doing the best she could in a difficult situation, so I put a hand on her shoulder. "Don't worry. I'll handle it. Could you give us a moment?"

Paige followed me into the living room as I settled Jessika and Jade on the couch, one daughter on either side of me.

"So," Jade asked between sniffles, "is it true, then? Do you have cancer, Daddy?"

"Yes," I said. "I wanted to wait to tell you until I knew for sure. We just got the call from the doctor a few minutes ago."

"Oh, Daddy!" they both cried in unison.

I held up my hand. "You need to know something very important." I waited until I had their full attention before continuing. "I plan to beat this."

"Can you?" Jessika asked with tears streaming down her face. "I mean, for real? Is it possible?"

"Yes, Sweetie," I said. "Anything is possible."

"But don't people die from cancer?" she asked.

"Sometimes. It's just that I don't plan to. I want to be around for a long, long time!"

"How are you going to do that?" Jade asked.

"I'm going to work hard, learn everything I can, and figure it out. And your mom is going to help me." Jade looked at Paige and then smiled at me. "I believe you, Daddy." Jessika looked a little less certain but nodded. "Me, too."

It's not that our daughters are gullible—it's that they wanted so desperately to believe it could be beaten. We all did. I didn't have any answers yet and was now, more than ever, under the gun to find them. The 800-pound gorilla had landed smack dab on my back. But I never doubted for a minute that we would find a way.

◆ ◆ ◆

I was eager to meet with Dr. A. the next day. It was the first step on my path to keeping the promise I'd made to my family. Research. If I was going to rid myself of this disease, I needed to learn as much as I could about it. Dr. A. had a plan, and I wanted to hear it.

"We're going to do everything we can for you," Dr. A. said, "but as I told you on the phone, there isn't a cure."

"Well then, Doc, what's the plan?" I asked.

"Well, if you start treatment immediately, you could live another five, maybe ten years. It's hard to know for sure."

Paige glared at him. "Is that really your idea of good news?"

"None of it is good news, but Non-Hodgkin's Lymphoma can be treated. That's all I meant," he said with a patient smile.

"So, what treatment plan do you have in mind?" I said.

"It's standard chemotherapy."

"But you're saying it can't cure me, just possibly reduce the tumors?"

He nodded. "Some of my patients are in remission."

"And what exactly does that mean?" Paige asked.

"Complete remission means that all the symptoms are gone, and there are no signs of cancer."

"Why isn't it a cure, then?" I asked.

"There might be a few cells left, cells that can't be picked up in follow-up tests, so the cancer could recur or reappear at a later date. You just can't ever be sure it's completely gone."

"So, remission is the best we can hope for?" Paige asked.

"Pretty much," Dr. A. said.

He handed me a clipboard. "Look, here are some pamphlets. Read them over, and then I'll need you to sign the consent form." Then he left the room to give us some privacy.

Paige and I silently read about the joys of chemo. It really wasn't something I was interested in exploring, but I wanted to inform myself about every option, even that one. According to the leaflets, chemo and radiation were the only acceptable treatment plans for my cancer. If I wanted to live at all, I needed to try to kill the cancer cells with chemicals.

"Hey, did you know that the first cancer chemo drug was actually mustard gas?" I asked.

"Oh, my! I had no idea," Paige said, shaking her head. "Not a great recommendation, is it?"

As I continued to read, I realized that there wasn't anything in the pamphlets that was changing my mind. If anything, it increased my aversion to chemo. I scanned the release form included on the clipboard Dr. A. had handed me.

Yeah, as if I'm going to sign that!

Before long, the red-haired nurse with a ready smile came in to collect the paperwork. She flipped through the forms, stopping at the one I was supposed to sign, and her smile faded.

"You forgot to sign this one," she said, handing it back to me.

"I didn't forget. I just didn't sign," I said, pushing the clipboard back toward her.

She looked at me with a puzzled expression.

Have you really never encountered a patient who refused to sign?

"But we can't give you chemo unless you sign the release."

Did she really think I'd missed that fact?

"I know. Look, I'm not convinced this is the right choice for me yet."

She opened and closed her mouth silently a few times before she left the room. Soon, Dr. A. came in and looked at me sternly. "My nurse tells me that you don't want to sign the release forms."

"Doc, my cousin's heart stopped when his nurse administered chemo, and my grandfather died soon after he was given the stuff. I'm just not sure I want to die from the treatment instead of the illness."

"I won't deny that some people don't survive chemo," Dr. A. said, "but it's rarer than you think." He sighed. "One thing's for sure: If you don't take the treatment, you will die. Chemo and radiation aren't pleasant treatments, but the alternative is death."

I studied him. I could tell he believed what he was saying. I liked Dr. A. He was an intelligent, professional doctor, and a nice, sincere guy to boot. It was just that I needed more time to try to find a better alternative. There had to be more than just chemo or death.

"How much time do I have, Doc?" I asked. "I mean, do you think I'll die tonight? Tomorrow? How about two weeks from now?"

"No, chances are you'll live at least that long," he said with a slight smile, "but you're going to start to get really sick very soon."

"Well, how long do I have then?"

He took out a handheld calculator and punched some numbers, working out some mysterious algorithm of death. Finally, he looked up at me and said, "If you take treatment, you can expect to live another five to ten years. However, if you don't start treatment, with your symptoms, I'd say you have less than ninety days to live, but that's only a guess."

There's an equation for life expectancy?

PAIGE

WHEN DR. A. FINISHED HIS MYSTERIOUS CALCULATIONS to determine how many years, days, hours, minutes I had left with my husband, he looked up and rang the death knell as if it were an acceptable thing to say.

Were doctors issued those things with their medical licenses?

This routine might have been very normal for him, but Rodney wasn't just any run-of-the-mill patient. This was my husband, the love of my life. I didn't care how many years Dr. A. had gone to school or how many patients he'd seen since he'd graduated. He had no right to just whip out a calculator, enter in some equation according to the stage of my husband's cancer, and compare it to other patients' statistics to see how long Rodney would live. Dr. A. had known him for only about a week, and there he was, giving my husband an expiration date.

Not on my watch!

My vision wavered for a moment, and then I leapt out of my chair, jumping over the examination table, like an Olympic pole-vaulter. As I cleared the bed, I snatched the stupid calculator out of his hands and threw it against the wall. It hit with such speed, it instantly shattered into a thousand pieces.

"There! That stupid thing won't ever calculate another death again!"

Dr. A. backed away from me, his eyes huge. He'd obviously never had to deal with anything like this before. "How dare you use that thing to tell someone as precious as my husband that he has only a few years to live!" I cried out. He stared at the ground. "I'm so . . . sorry," he stuttered.

I would have felt sorry for Dr. A., but I knew he'd continue to run the same calculations on other patients if I didn't put a stop to it once and for all. He had to see the error of his ways.

The poor man started mumbling medical technobabble, hoping to confuse me, but I was no longer mesmerized by his blinding white coat or the framed medical degrees on his wall.

"How dare you compare my husband to all the other patients, who smoke and drink, among other things?" By this time, I was so worked up I began to spew fire with each word. I couldn't help it. I managed to singe his eyebrows a little. "Have some respect!"

When he looked up at me, something in his expression had changed. He finally seemed to realize he wasn't talking to Mr. and Mrs. Joe Average. No, he was beginning to see we were people who actually thought for themselves. He was talking to Superman and his wife.

"Now, Doctor, give us a real treatment plan, something that actually might cure my man!" I stared intently into his eyes, trying to pull the information from him.

"Paige!" Rodney's voice penetrated my haze. I continued to stare at the doctor, willing him to give me some measure of hope for a cure.

"Paige. Paige!" Rodney shouted.

The daydream that I had so carefully constructed fell apart. My eyes focused back on the room, and I looked around. The doctor was gone, and Rodney looked more than a little worried.

I kept my voice casual. "Yes?"

"Are you okay?" Rodney asked. "You kind of checked out there for a minute."

Why are you always worried about me?

"I'm fine," I said. "What did I miss?"

"Dr. A. agreed to give me two weeks to research options. He asked me not to wait too long, though."

I nodded. "I'll help you."

"I'm counting on it!" he said. "Are you ready to go home?"

"Yeah!" I jumped up.

I've never been more ready.

I looked around the room for any trace of the shattered calculator but found none. I frowned, realizing that Dr. A. would be using it again on another patient before too long.

Drat!

CHAPTER 3

Searching for Solutions

RODNEY

THE MOMENT WE ARRIVED HOME FROM THE DOCTOR, we made a beeline for our computers. We began researching, quickly discovering that the Internet was full of information, though not all of it correct or helpful. There were tons of stories and opinions, many of which conflicted. Fortunately, we were both dedicated and motivated. We had only two weeks to accomplish a mammoth task.

No pressure.

Paige started by reviewing all the standard sites, reading what the Leukemia and Lymphoma Society and the American Cancer Society promoted. I glanced through their material but was disgusted by their lack of alternatives to chemotherapy and radiation. The standard approach was a one-note song, and I needed alternatives. It wasn't hard to find other treatment plans for cancer, but some sources discussed some pretty outlandish concepts.

As I was searching the Internet, a friend from Texas called. He told me about an alternative treatment a friend of his had used with success. When I hung up the phone, I asked Paige, "Have you ever heard of Black Salve?"

"Uh, no. What is it?"

"It's a combination of herbs that you put on a tumor to draw it out through the skin. It sounds pretty fascinating and gross at the same time. Apparently, a friend of Doug's used it with some success. He's pulled out something like twenty to thirty tumors already!"

"Rodney, you know we need to check out both sides of everything, right?"

"Yes, but I just want to make sure we don't dismiss something just because it's unconventional."

"Don't worry. I'm with you on that."

I continued looking for the downside to this unorthodox treatment. I quickly typed the term into my search engine and pulled up a slew of pages. Some sites raved about the salve, claiming that it was a magical, miracle cancer cure. Several patients reported that they were able to extract tumors through their skin after only a week or two, but they all said it was extremely painful.

Other websites warned that it was dangerous pseudo-science. One in particular was quite graphic. "Yikes!" I cried out in horror as I read over an article about a woman from Florida who'd gone to a plastic surgeon complaining about excess skin under her nose.

"Paige, look at this," I said, horrified. She leaned over next to me to read the rest of the story.

The woman was diagnosed with cancer, and a health practitioner gave her a black salve he'd made himself. Finally, after suffering for more than a week with the stuff, she went to the emergency room. By that time, her nose had burned almost completely off. The pictures shown were startling and disgusting.

In another case, it seems they put it on a neck tumor, and the reaction spread to her face. It just violently goes after tumors wherever it can find them.

"That's a bit terrifying and seems hard to control."

"If your tumors are all localized, it might just work. Hey, it's worth a try. I'm game if you are!" Paige said deviously.

Slowly looking up at her as if she had lost her mind, I said, "What if I have a tumor that we don't know about? That stuff might pull all kinds of things out of my body. No way am I trying that!"

Paige seemed to be getting a kick out of my agitation and said, "If those tumors don't start shrinking pretty soon, I'm going to black salve you in the middle of the night while you're sleeping!"

"You wouldn't!"

She shrugged and looked back at her screen, stifling a giggle. "We'll see."

"Guess I'll be sleeping with one eye open," I muttered.

I knew just how serious she was about killing those things. She hated them with a passion.

Paige and I continued to search and found all sorts of interesting stories and opinions. Some seemed somewhat plausible, and others seemed downright weird. One theory was that cancer starts with Candida, a fungus. We found a site that recommended oil of oregano, and another claimed that baking soda would bring about a cure. One guy said just eating asparagus every day will get rid of cancer.

If only the solution were that easy.

There was a huge amount of information on the subject of cancer, so much, in fact, that it made my head spin. Still, I was determined to wade through it all, view every site, read every opinion on the subject that anyone had to say. I'm good at speed-reading and can weed out the strange from the potentially helpful without too much trouble.

"Here's one," I said.

"Whatcha got?" Paige asked.

"Have you run across anything on hyperthermia yet?"

She shook her head. "Isn't that where you freeze the body?"

"No, that's hypothermia. This is the opposite, where you expose the body to high temperatures to kill cancer cells. They're using it in Germany with some success."

Paige quickly began researching the treatment. "This says it's often used along with chemo and radiation."

"Not always. I bet you're on a medico site, right?"

"Yeah," she said.

"When it's used with radiation, it's called Thermoradiotherapy, but it's been very successful on its own with certain kinds of cancers."

We continued to research and read until we were too exhausted to continue. When I went to bed that night, I had trouble getting the various pictures and stories out of my head.

PAIGE

THE NEXT MORNING, WHILE RODNEY CONTINUED TO SURF the Internet, I went out for groceries and ran into an old friend at the checkout counter. It's funny how people come out of the woodwork to tell you all about their friends and relatives who have or had cancer. As it turned out, though, this guy's cousin had Non-Hodgkin's Lymphoma, which was a wild coincidence. He told me that she'd gone to Germany to do hyperthermia, which had worked well.

I couldn't wait to get home to share the news with Rodney. When I relayed all the information to him, he looked relieved.

"Yeah, but my friend said it was super expensive, especially since you'd have to go to Germany. His cousin's loaded, so it wasn't a problem for her."

"Well, it's definitely something to think about. We'll include it as an alternative treatment option."

RODNEY

I PRINTED OUT AN INFORMATION SHEET ABOUT IT and put it in the white folder, which held all of our cancer paperwork. I had various treatment options organized and tabbed already, but nothing stood out as the perfect solution. Not yet.

Over the next few days, Paige and I continued to cull through articles on the Internet. We learned that cancer is really a group of diseases which have one thing in common: uncontrolled cell growth. Lymphomas are classed as blood cancers, in which too many lymphocytes (white blood cells) fill up the lymph nodes, causing them to swell. In normal, healthy bodies, new cells are created every day, with a predetermined lifespan, from a few hours to a few weeks.

When cells have fulfilled that time, they commit suicide, dying naturally. This process is called apoptosis or programmed cell death. If new cells are continually born and no cells die off, cancer is the result.

We found more information about chemotherapy, but it wasn't encouraging. It seems that medical doctors are severely limited in what they have to offer victims of cancer. If they can cut it out, burn it out, or poison it with high-priced pharmaceutical drugs, they are safely within the rigid confines of the AMA. To deviate is professional suicide. The concepts suggested by Hippocrates, the Father of Medicine, "First, do no harm" and "Let food be thy medicine" seem to be totally foreign to current modalities.

Well, we'd just have to find something elsewhere. Most of the sites looked familiar, with similar information, but, in time, Paige found something new. Something that caught my attention, too.

On the screen was a site about a company called Rational Therapeutics.

"Hey, this might be something. This company has the surgeon overnight your tumor right after the biopsy. Then they test various chemo agents on it to see which will work for your type of cancer."

We wondered why the doctor hadn't told us about that. Wouldn't he want to test it for the right drug instead of shooting blindly in the dark?

"If you're going to go the chemo route, that sounds like the best way to approach it," I said.

Paige decided to take a break, so she stepped out into the back yard to call Monica, an old family friend, who is an anesthesiologist. Coming back into the house, she quickly summarized the call to me while my eyes were still glued to the computer. Monica had related that she had a patient who had lymphoma, too. That patient received a stem-cell transplant and wound up in remission. She seemed pretty excited about it.

Paige was committed to helping me fully explore all my options, getting all the data possible to help me make a final decision. But I could tell that she was feeling pressure, because both Dr. A. and Monica insisted we were wasting precious moments when I should be getting treatments.

"Monica was concerned that you might opt for a charlatan approach, which is what she calls anything that isn't conventional medicine. She was pretty convincing. I mean, we only have one shot to get this right, right?"

I could tell that Paige was trying to be objective and lay everything out for me. It was a fine balance, and I could see her concern. No hysterics. What a wife. She's the best.

But I was one step ahead.

"First of all, they give you a stem-cell transplant only if you try chemotherapy and it doesn't work. It's the last option for that treatment. Do you have any idea what the odds are of surviving a stem-cell transplant?"

"Well, uh, no—not really."

"Well, I do. I looked up the statistics for stem-cell transplants. Ten to twenty-five percent of the people live for only five years, if they survive the operation. Some websites give it only a four percent success rate. Four, Paige! Not exactly the odds we're looking for here."

"Right."

"Yeah, so maybe I can get five years. That's if I manage to survive, which is a big 'if.' That's not nearly enough time for me. I'm not willing to bet my life on those odds!"

"No, I'm not either."

My symptoms were ramping up. I was no longer just a tired guy with lumps. The sweats, nausea, fever, and general sickness were telling me that the situation was urgent. My disease had moved from "indolent" to an aggressive large B-Cell Lymphoma, a much more virulent form.

Finding a nugget of knowledge in all the available data wasn't going to be easy. It was frustrating to wade through all the garbage on the Internet. Too many sites were just so unhelpful. Everyone with an opinion and a domain name could write whatever they wanted. And if we unwittingly used just the right keywords, wacky notions would pop up on our search.

"Everybody seems to be an expert these days. Thanks, Google!"

"Isn't that the truth."

Being equally determined, we doggedly trudged on. We had learned too much to turn back now. There just had to be something out there that had a plausible track record and wasn't hocus-pocus.

Paige asked if I would talk to Monica, in the spirit of research. I agreed, so that evening we sent all of my paperwork for her to look over, so she'd have some idea of the specifics of my situation.

PAIGE

AS I SAT NEXT TO RODNEY AND SURFED THE NET, I thought about what Monica had said. Her words filled my mind to the point where I couldn't see the screen in front of me. *"You're wasting precious time. He has to start chemo now."* Her words rang in my ears. I was scared out of my wits, and she was making it worse. "I'm going to bed," I said, realizing that I wasn't going to be much more use that night.

Not that I expected to sleep. Sleep had eluded me from the day Rodney first went to the doctor. I got no more than an hour's sleep most nights. Mainly I watched him sleep. His rhythmic, sonorous breathing was reassuring, and I couldn't bear the thought that I might miss the moment it stopped. Besides, my mind was flooded with thoughts of pathology reports, CT scans, and biopsies.

The next day, Rodney talked to Monica. Listening to his side of the phone call, I could tell that Monica was continuing to push traditional medicine, which wasn't sitting well with Rodney. At the end of the call, he looked frustrated and tired.

RODNEY

PAIGE'S FRIEND, MONICA, WAS AN M.D. with considerable experience, and her specialty was anesthesiology. She saw it all.

"You have to start chemo," she said after we exchanged a polite greeting.

I sighed in frustration and then bit my tongue and counted to ten. I didn't want to be rude, so I chose my words carefully.

"I'm not sure I want to do that."

"You really have no choice," she said.

Is it my imagination, or does she sound irritated?

"Respectfully, I disagree. I had two relatives who died while on chemo."

"I'm sorry to hear that," she said, her voice softening. "I really am. But you can't just blame the drug. After all, your family members were sick."

"I know," I said. "And that's a valid point, but from everything I've read, chemo is a poison."

"That's why it works. That's why it kills the cancer." She paused and then said, "Look, I have a patient who had the exact same cancer as you, and he did well on chemo."

"What happened?" I asked, my curiosity piqued.

"They did heavy chemo and then a stem-cell transplant," she said.

"So, the chemo didn't work. It was the stem cells."

"No, it was the combination."

I thought for a moment, questioning the wisdom of seeking a second opinion from another medical doctor. They all seemed to have the same opinion about how to approach this illness. They appeared to be rigidly disease oriented and locked into prescribing synthetic prescription drugs that just treat symptoms and don't dig into causes. Frequently they merely mask the symptoms and are like a band-aid on a gaping wound. If the drugs are stopped, the illness comes back with a vengeance.

The medical establishment is like the Pied Piper. Patients are expected to blindly follow, even when outcomes are not good. The stranglehold that the drug companies have on the entire process is evident in the training that medical students receive. Young medics are indoctrinated right from the start to believe that their way is the only way. Anything else is foolish and contemptible. The drug companies openly, actively, and without shame sponsor ads in textbooks and in numerous other ways have infiltrated medical schools. And chemotherapy is a huge moneymaker for them.

"I think there are viable alternatives. I just need time to explore them."

"What sort of alternatives?" Her words sounded strained, and I could imagine she was struggling to keep the derision out of her voice. To give her credit, she didn't sound too condescending.

"I'd rather not say yet, because Paige and I have just begun our research, but if you'd like, I'll share with you what we find."

"Yes, I'm interested, but please don't take too long," she said. "You should really start on chemo immediately. I hope your research brings you to that conclusion."

Have you been talking to Dr. A.?

"Sure, I'll let you know what I decide."

I hung up the phone and saw Paige's pretty face etched all over with worry and fear. It was formidable to hear the authority figures in our lives declare that my death was imminent. It was extremely intimidating to have the educated and trained medicos all in sync, repeating the same old saw. Despite any arguments that might favor chemo, or who made them, I knew that my courageous, bold, and outspoken wife would think for herself. She would not wilt in the face of opposition. She was adamant that it was my body—and my treatment choice.

I was confident that, in the end, Paige would support whatever path I chose. Still, I wanted her to be an active participant in the decision-making process.

After I finished the rundown of my conversation with Monica, Paige nodded and said, "It does seem like some people do well on chemo."

"But they're never completely cancer free," I reminded her. "Even Dr. A. admitted that, and, from everything I've read so far, the medical community concurs. Chemo doesn't cure anything. It just knocks down tumors. And they tend to come back."

She twisted the ends of her long hair. "Yeah, I know."

"The thing I can't wrap my wits around is why chemo would ever be the first line of therapy. It just didn't make much sense to me to poison a system that is obviously full of poison already. It obliterates the immune system, making it hard for anything else to work. There's no fallback. And what about quality of life? Another problem is that the body builds up a resistance to the treatment, so subsequent treatments are less effective. I'd rather die naturally than be poisoned to death."

I gathered her into a hug. "Hey, why don't we get out of the house and go to the bookstore tonight? We can do some light reading on cancer."

Paige rolled her eyes. "Light reading, my foot."

"Well, maybe the girls can find some fun books to read."

"Actually, there are a few titles I wanted to look up, now that you mention it." She stretched in her chair and rubbed her eyes with the back of her hand. "Plus, I'd love a break from the computer."

PAIGE

We packed the kids into the truck and headed to a huge brick-and-mortar bookstore with overstuffed chairs and a coffee bar where you could get smoothies, coffee, and anything that would satisfy a sweet tooth. Two weeks ago, I would have stopped in for some hot chocolate with chocolate drizzled atop the mound of whipped cream, but now I saw that little coffee bar as a cancer café, selling everything that was totally unhealthy for you. Boy, how my perception had changed in just a few short days.

Bypassing the sweet temptations, we made our way down a long aisle labeled "Health." As luck would have it, there was a reading area with four comfy chairs all situated around a table close by.

Rodney pulled a few books off the shelf and plopped down in one of the caramel-colored chairs. I made my way to the kids' section with Jessika and Jade, who seemed relieved that they didn't have to drown themselves in the misery of cancer research.

It didn't take long for them to find books to interest them. When Jade found a cute book that taught how to make friendship bracelets, her eyes lit up.

"It even has yarn so I can start making one now!"

She looked so happy that I wanted to buy five copies for her.

"Can I get it?" she asked.

"Absolutely!" I replied. "But, let's get a few others, just in case you get bored with that one."

"Wow," she said. After another ten minutes, she had picked out several other books.

"Oh, Momma—this is so cool! I can learn how to do braids, tie-dye stuff, and all sorts of things."

"Those look like good choices," I said, pulling the top few off the stack to ease her burden. "You can look over all of them and pick out a few to buy. Come on—bring them over to where Daddy's sitting."

I saw that Rodney was already poring over the books piled all around him. When we arrived, Jade put her books down on the circular table in the center of the group of chairs.

"Now, Jessika, let's head over and see what we can find for you," I said, waving to Rodney, whose head was already buried in another book. Jade sat in front of Rodney, happily playing with her braid book.

Jessika had always loved to read. When we would ground her for acting up, we quickly learned not to relegate her to her room, because she loved to curl up with a good book. Instead, we'd tell her she wasn't allowed to read a book for pleasure until her punishment was up. That always achieved the desired effect.

Walking over to the teen section, she reviewed every book on the shelves, meticulously reading the back covers, looking for the perfect one to read. When we walked back, Jessika fell into the fourth chair, and Jade didn't seem to even notice us. She had deserted her chair, opting to sit on the floor, with her books fanned out around her. She looked to be reading three at the same time.

Good—they're distracted. My turn!

I walked over to the cancer section, immediately feeling overwhelmed by the number of books on the subject. I began to pull random books off the shelves until I had two dozen or so. I chose a few on cancer diets, a couple on natural cures, and some on chemotherapy. A few other patrons glanced my way, as I wasn't exactly in stealth mode about the subject of my research.

Staggering under the weight of the books, I made it back to Rodney, unloading the tower onto the central table. A few tumbled to the floor, causing Jade to jump. She looked up at me with her large Bambi eyes, flinging her right hand to her chest for emphasis.

Once she went back to her reading, I grabbed the first book from the top of my stack and started skimming through it. It wasn't very helpful, so I picked out the next. As I read, I got some insights into concepts that I could research further at home on the Internet. I didn't get too far through my pile before the girls were ready to leave.

RODNEY

ONE BOOK IN PARTICULAR JUMPED OUT AT ME: *Questioning Chemotherapy*, by Dr. Ralph Moss. As I glanced through it, I realized that one of the problems with chemo was that it harmed the good cells as well as the cancerous ones. Dr. Moss made the point that these drugs are very toxic. He went on, stating that chemo has never really been proven to be effective on some cancers.

If the immune system is the first line of defense against germs, filtering out harmful intruders, how could it be helpful to poison it further?

He also explored the reason why the drugs for chemo were so popular, and it wasn't pretty. It seemed that the pharmaceutical industry was cleaning up financially with cancer. Hard to believe that anyone would try to make money off the suffering of others, but it seemed clear to me that the drug companies didn't have cancer patients' best interests at heart. I bought the book and handed it to Paige as soon as I'd finished reading it.

"Read this, and tell me what you think. I'm interested in your take."

She read it cover to cover over the next few days. After that, she veered away from the medically oriented cancer sites and began concentrating on the more-alternative options. We both put our feelers out amongst our friends, looking for other solutions, ones that had a proven track record.

Dr. Moss also confirmed what I had been reading elsewhere. Chemotherapy wasn't a cure but a treatment to shrink tumors, which might buy a little time for the patient, if any at all.

Cancer doctors have to have a killer instinct to kill cancer. Often, they very nearly kill their patients in the process. With all the devastating side effects, from hair loss and vomiting, along with the distinct possibility that it could cause other cancers and even death, this treatment plan wasn't a good option for me.

Another drawback was that chemotherapy was far too expensive, something we could never afford. We had no health insurance, so the cost was prohibitive, even with a discount, which Dr. A. had offered us.

CHAPTER 4

Essiac Tea

PAIGE

THE NEXT NIGHT, I RECEIVED AN UNEXPECTED CALL from a friend, and when she heard about Rodney's plight, she suggested a special tea. At first I groaned inwardly, thinking it was just another bogus cure, but after she'd finished explaining how her dad had beaten cancer using this tea, I did some research.

It was called Essiac tea, named after a nurse in Canada. Actually, it was her last name spelled backwards. Rene Caisse had devoted her life to successfully treating patient after patient with this tea. I ordered it online, figuring it couldn't hurt. I also ordered special amber glass bottles for storing the liquid, because direct sunlight could reduce its effectiveness.

When it arrived, I tore open the box and followed the instructions to the letter. It had a really strange odor, which I found oddly comforting. If it'd had no smell, I probably wouldn't have trusted it.

To brew it, I had to use the only stainless-steel pot we had, because other metals can leech into the tea. Fortunately, the prepared tea had a shelf-life of two weeks, so at least I didn't have to brew the stuff daily. I was curious about the ingredients. A year before her death, Caisse released the secret formula to a company in Toronto, so they could continue to manufacture it. It was a blend of Sheep Sorrel Root (the main ingredient purported to cure cancer), Burdock Root, Slippery Elm Inner Bark, and Indian Rhubarb Root.

I followed the instructions carefully, feeling like a drug dealer, mixing all these strange herbs together, and let it steep overnight. I wondered how it would come out and hoped Rodney could stomach it.

The next morning I was up bright and early, pouring Rodney his first sample of the tea. I watched him closely. It didn't take long for me to get a response.

He wrinkled his nose. "It has a weird smell. I can't describe it. It's not like any tea I've ever smelled before."

It would take some getting used to, especially since he couldn't add any sweetener, as sugar is said to feed the cancer.

"Ugh!" he cried out after swallowing a single gulp. "This stuff tastes terrible!" I decided to try it, too. So often our palates were diametrically opposed, and I had broader experience with strange tastes than he had.

"I kind of like it."

"You would, you tree hugger. You thrive on this type of stuff. I, however, eat for enjoyment," he chided.

"And look where that got you."

To his credit, Rodney was willing to try anything and everything that made sense. The tea, antioxidants, and another supplement called Poly MVA were part of his daily efforts to get better. Amazingly, his night sweats stopped within a week. We couldn't believe it. They had come on so suddenly, creating such misery, frightening us half to death. And now they were completely gone.

It completely baffled Dr. A. as well. He said the night sweats shouldn't come and go like that.

We went to work at our day jobs and then continued our research after dinner. When ten-thirty rolled around, I reminded him that, if he were to get well, he needed to get at least eight hours of sleep. He was asleep as soon as his head hit the pillow. I was so jealous. The tornado that had wrapped itself around me and was sucking me dry made sleep elusive. Finally, as the sun was about to rise, I dropped off for a few winks.

All too soon, I awoke to a clicking sound. Peeking my head over the covers, I listened intently for a while, in an attempt to identify the strange noise. Finally, I yanked off the comforter and strolled out of our bedroom. As I got closer, I realized that Rodney must be typing away on the computer.

As I made my way to the dining room, I caught a glimpse of my bed hair. I could definitely pass for Medusa's twin sister. Grinning, I sauntered up to Rodney, plopped myself on his lap, gave him a big kiss, and waited for his reaction to my hair.

He looked at me affectionately. "Good morning, sunshine!"

He lifted a hand and attempted to smooth my unruly hair.

I laughed. "After almost fifteen years of marriage, you're still trying to tame it?"

He continued his research without letup, as I gave the house a thorough cleaning. After a few hours, when it got too quiet, I tiptoed back to Rodney. He was sitting quietly in front of the computer, clearly distraught.

"What happened?" I asked.

"I've been following a blog about a lady with a young son who's very ill," he said, his voice quiet. "She writes while he sleeps."

"How's he doing?" I asked, not sure if I wanted to know the answer.

"The family had exhausted all their treatment options, so they opted for a stem-cell transplant. I just logged in to see how he was doing today and found out that he died last night. I can't believe it. I was really hoping that he'd beat the odds and make it. He was so young, and the mom was so optimistic."

"I'm so sorry," I said, reaching up to rub the back of his head. "That's so incredibly sad."

I couldn't imagine what it must have felt like to read about so many cancer patients who didn't make it. It couldn't be good for him. "How long have you been on these forums and websites?"

He thought for a moment. "Probably about two weeks."

"Would you say that most of the patients are doing well? Or that they are in pretty bad shape?"

"Pretty bad," he replied with a sigh. "They all seem to be on chemo and talk about how horrible they feel. Most are losing their hair, can't eat, and seem to be vomiting all the time. They're all miserable, but none of them feel like they can stop doing chemo, because they just don't think they have any other options. Their doctors all advise them to just stay the course, but a lot of them just want to stop, and some do stop."

"I can't imagine what they're going through," I whispered.

"It seems like throwing up is a daily ritual for most of them."

"Oh, Baby," I said, continuing to rub his head gently. "I know how much you hate vomiting. Look, why don't you take a break from these depressing sites?"

"But I need to do all the research I can," he said. "I need to try to find out what people are doing to fight cancer. I need to learn what's working."

"I know. I get that, and I agree, but maybe you should stop reading about the chemo patients. After all, you've pretty much ruled that one out."

He sighed. "But I promised Dr. A. to research all angles before making my decision."

"I don't think anyone can accuse you of short-cutting that process," I said with a shake of my head. "You've done your research. I think it's time to stop visiting these forums and websites where people aren't surviving. They can't possibly be motivating you."

He looked at me intently." Yeah, you're right. These sites are just upsetting me. And a lot of the people who are dying aren't any older than I am. Actually, some are quite a bit younger!"

"The kids are the ones who get me the most," I said quietly.

"Me, too. It's all I can think of."

"Just stop going to those sites. Please."

"But I should be able to take it," he said.

"Reading over the last dying words of people on chemo isn't going to help you. Not even a little."

He thought about it for a moment. "You're right. There's got to be something out there that's not based on a toxic poison that will give me a fighting chance."

"Well, if there is, you'll be the one to find it." I leaned over to give him a kiss.

"Thanks, Sweetie. I needed that."

"Who loves you?" I asked.

"You do!" he replied.

"That's right, and don't you ever forget it!" I smiled, walking out of the room. I'd made a point of asking that question to the girls on a regular basis, even when they were very young. It was important to me that they always knew and never doubted that I loved them. Now, I realized I should include Rodney in that ritual as well. He needed to hear that I loved him just as much as the girls did.

Rodney cut back on the chemo cancer patient sites and focused his attention on nontraditional therapies. He and I quickly became more encouraged by what we found. There were a surprisingly large number of patients who were doing pretty well with alternative methods.

RODNEY

I REALIZED THAT, ALTHOUGH RESEARCHING on the Internet was easy, I needed to talk to real people as well, so I interviewed several chemo patients. A few were from Dr. A's office, while others were people I personally knew. I quickly learned that many patients who survived the chemo and radiation treatment suffered from a recurrence of the disease later. Their bodies had been weakened by the drugs, so the chemo was often less effective the second time around. I concluded that the body must build up a resistance to the treatment.

A friend of a friend referred me to an elderly gentleman, someone who had survived cancer. I was excited to talk to him and find out what he had done to beat the seemingly unbeatable illness.

When I picked up the phone, I wasn't sure exactly what I'd say to the man. After all, I hardly knew him, and here I was about to ask him a slew of very personal questions.

"Thank you for speaking with me," I said carefully, not really knowing where to start.

"No problem, young man!" His voice sounded so full of life. "Anthony tells me that you'd like to talk to me about my lung cancer I had a few years back."

"I hadn't realized it was that recent."

"Yes, I'd had it for years before that, but, at one point, the doctors called it quits with chemo. They said my body wouldn't handle another dose, not at my age."

"Wow," I said. "So, what did you do?"

"At first, I was at a loss. I went home and kind of prepared to die. It was my son who kicked me in the butt and talked me into fighting back. He started making me these concoctions to drink. And they did the trick!"

"What was in them?"

"To be honest, I don't know. My son put them together. I could find out for you, though."

"That would be great!'

"I can't promise that it will work for you, though. But I'm convinced there are a number of good, workable natural treatments. My advice is to research everything available, figure out what you want to do, and commit to that."

"I'm with you on that," I said. "May I ask, how old are you?"

"I'll be eighty-three next spring," he replied, and I could practically see him grinning on the other end of the phone. "And I still walk three miles every day."

"Whoa! That's amazing! You're amazing!"

"Son, just remember. If I can do it, so can you."

When I hung up with him, I felt re-energized. He was quite an inspiration. Following his advice, I continued to research options. The more people I spoke to, the more convinced I became that chemotherapy was not a good solution for me. Plus, it was clear that if I chose that route, there was no going back. My body would be too weak afterwards to try anything else.

PAIGE

RODNEY ACTUALLY LAUGHED WHILE TALKING to this man. It astounded me that this complete and total stranger was having such an amazing effect on my husband. I closed my eyes, relishing the music of his laughter. It had been so long since I'd heard that sound come from my beloved.

After Rodney hung up the phone, he looked rejuvenated. A second wind had come over him, inspiring him to go into the garage, turn on the treadmill, and start running. He didn't take it easy or warm up, either. He ran like a stallion that had been released from his confines and wouldn't be harnessed.

I don't know what motivated him, if it was the extreme stress from such a dire situation, or the excitement, encouragement, and hope that this man had given him. It didn't matter. All that mattered was that Rodney was engaged and ready for the fight of his life. This newfound hope might just be Rodney's muse.

Later that evening, hoping to find something simple, something that wouldn't be too complicated to follow, he stumbled upon a great-sounding website, based in Florida. They seemed to have an FDA-approved cure for cancer, which involved taking only a single pill a day. Looking over the testimonials, it looked like it could cure anyone within six weeks.

Was this what we had been looking for?

CHAPTER 5

Big Pimpin' Pappy's Fake Cancer Cure

RODNEY

THE WEBSITE FOR THIS ONE-PILL WONDER had many testimonials from medical professionals. More than a dozen doctors were featured, complete with photographs and credentials, along with their recommendations to use this product.

In addition, countless testimonials from patients were posted, people who had used these pills, with miraculous success. Each piece included a photograph of the patient, showing them looking happy and healthy.

I looked over the pages, searching for some mention of side effects. There were none—no downside. The pill appeared to have a remarkable success rate, but I wasn't ready to rush out and buy it. I needed to look into it a bit more.

The first thing I noticed was that the active ingredient was Camptosar, a drug used in chemotherapy. Instead of injections, this company had apparently found a way to put it into capsules.

Poring over the site, numerous patients stated that it was painless and easy, and at only $150 a bottle, was much more cost effective than many other treatment plans. I could actually afford that.

I was excited by the prospect of being cured within six weeks. It was a huge improvement over all the other treatments out there, which typically took far longer. The idea of the wonder pill really looked appealing and sounded legitimate. Except that all my warning bells were sounding in a cacophony of noise in my mind. It simply didn't make any sense. Nothing on the site matched anything else I'd read. It just wasn't logical. Yes, I was desperate to find an easy cure, but I also knew better than to fall for a scam.

Since the site mentioned it was an FDA-approved drug, I clicked on the link they provided. I immediately noticed that the web address didn't match the official Food and Drug Administration site, and I couldn't get to the site through search engines—only by clicking on the link.

More warning bells.

However, before I completely ruled this cure out, I picked up the phone and called the FDA. They immediately referred me over to the FBI, who told me that this company was under investigation.

Of course, it is!

They took my statement, asked me if I had had any dealings with the company, and warned me to stay clear. The owner of the site was none other than the notorious pimp, Arthur Vanmoor, also known as "Big Pimping Pappy." A Dutch national operating out of Pompano Beach, Florida, Vanmoor made millions from escort services each year.

In the last month alone, he had sold almost four thousand bottles of the phony cancer-cure pills, which worked out to about $500,000.

How many people had died as a result of this website?

Researching Vanmoor, I learned he had been busted for racketeering a number of times. Unfortunately, he'd fought back with legal battles, hiring attorneys to sue the police department. He even went so far as to hire a private detective to harass a particular officer.

Big Pimping Pappy had fifty escorts working for him and spent $800,000 a year on ads, making who knows how many millions of dollars a year. Public records showed that he declared $6 million to the IRS the previous year, so my guess would be he actually made much more. He had hundreds of company names, all of which funneled back to a tiny hole-in-the-wall office in Pompano Beach.

The pills he sold contained an unknown substance, and no one ever figured out what he was putting in them. The makers of Camptosar commented that it was impossible to put that particular drug in pill form, as it could only be injected.

Wanting to make sure that no one else fell for this scam, I contacted several media outlets, and Fox News took the story. I detailed everything I had learned about Big Pimping Pappy and his miracle drug.

Douglas Kennedy, an investigative reporter for *The Big Story with John Gibson* of Fox, sent out a camera crew to interview me, asking me all sorts of questions about my family and diagnosis. When they arrived, they asked if they could rearrange our furniture and some pictures to set the stage for the interview. They also set up huge lights and positioned the camera right in front of where I'd be sitting.

We set up a phone next to me and put it on speaker so I could hear the questions from Douglas Kennedy and respond while they filmed. After the interview was finished, they wanted to film Paige and me in different settings. Since I'm an avid Bible reader, they wanted a shot of Paige and me lying down together reading the Bible. The other was the family playing a board game together, which, unfortunately, didn't make the cut. The whole ordeal took a couple of hours. They aired the story in two parts.

I was featured in the segment about the cancer scam. In order to make the story more interesting and dramatic, they reported that I had fallen prey to the scam. Although I hadn't actually purchased anything from the company, I could see how reporting that I had been duped might be more sensational and attention grabbing.

The other segment delved into the seedy life of Big Pimping Pappy. The reporter visited the escort office in Florida and was physically and verbally assaulted by the woman running the front desk. It definitely made for good news.

I was relieved to learn that, in December 2005, the United States Attorney's Office issued a restraining order against Vanmoor. As it turned out, he had miraculous cures for migraine headaches and the flu as well. He fled the country but was extradited from the Netherlands in 2007 to face his crimes.

In the end, Vanmoor was sentenced to 210 months in prison. He was also convicted of 19 separate counts of fraud. He wouldn't be running that scam on anyone else anymore.

The entire experience gave me a renewed confidence that I could sift through all the data on the Internet, uncover the right treatment, and not fall for the cons. I devoted all my time to discovering a treatment plan that would work for me. I didn't have much time, but I did have hope.

CHAPTER 6

The Book

RODNEY

IN ORDER TO ATTACK IT FULLY, I NEEDED TO LEARN the correct classification of my cancer. Treatment-plan options would vary, depending on the cancer's stage. The higher the stage, the more intensive the plan.

The first stage of Non-Hodgkin's Lymphoma is when it is localized in a single lymph node. The second and third stages are more advanced, showing that the disease has spread into other areas. And the fourth is widespread, entering into the bone marrow.

Based on the biopsy, Dr. A. had classified me as a Stage IIIB. I was deemed "B" because I was showing visible signs of the disease, like weight loss, fevers, night sweats, etc. Since he couldn't confirm that I *wasn't* Stage IV without testing my bone marrow, he urged me to undergo a bone-marrow biopsy. It wasn't *impossible* to rebound after Stage IV, but my chances of surviving would lessen.

When Dr. A. called me to schedule the biopsy, he said, "We're able to do this one without general anesthesia, if you'd prefer."

"Definitely. Thanks, Doc," I said.

After arriving at the doctor's office, I was immediately called back to the patient-exam room. I took my position on the exam table, and

Paige sat in a chair next to me. Our friend Brad, who came along for support, stayed back in the waiting room.

"This place is freezing," I said.

"I know." She glanced nervously around the room. "They say it discourages the growth of germs."

"It'll be okay."

She sighed. "Yeah, I know."

Dr. A. came in, wearing a blue shirt and khaki pants.

"Hey, Rodney."

"Hey, Doc."

"You can go ahead and get changed into this fancy man-dress," he said. "Then we'll get started."

I nodded and looked over at the tray of instruments his red-haired nurse had brought into the room. The eye-popping syringe was enough to make me shudder. It looked like he'd stolen it from some horror-movie set, where a deranged doctor was bent on extracting information from his victim.

"Is that what you're going to use on me today?" I asked, looking at a needle about eight inches long. It was as thick as a spaghetti noodle, with a handle at one end.

"Yeah," he said. "I'll need to use a lot of numbing agent on your hip."

After he injected me with the numbing agent, which I assumed was Novocain, he left the room while we waited for the agent to take full effect. When he returned 15 minutes later with the red-haired nurse in tow, he felt around a bit. "Looks like we're ready to start. You'll feel an intense pressure as I work to penetrate the bone. I'm not going to lie to you. Once I hit the marrow, it's going to be painful. The anesthetic won't work on the inside."

I nodded, feeling a little woozy. Dr. A. inserted the needle and proceeded to screw it round and round, like he was trying to open a bottle of wine. I lay there, gritting my teeth together, gripping the protective paper I was lying on.

Dr. A. struggled over me for 30 minutes, panting and sweating, working to get the needle through the bone. He had to put his entire weight into it as he drilled into my hip.

PAIGE

RODNEY WAS ADAMANT ABOUT STAYING AWAKE, but there was no way *I'd* ever consider going through a bone-marrow biopsy awake. I would have fled the room the moment I caught a glimpse of that needle. As a little girl, and even as an adult, my dentist had to hide the Novocain needle behind his back so that I couldn't see it. And that's a small thing compared to the instrument Dr. A. was using on Rodney.

Nobody should have to go through this.

After about half an hour, a red-faced Dr. A. asked, "Are you okay? Are you feeling anything?"

Rodney grunted that he was okay. "The pressure's intense, but there's no pain."

"Man, you're certainly giving me a workout. I've never seen another patient with bones as strong as yours!" It was true. Rodney's dentist had told him that his teeth were super strong. After he was diagnosed with cancer, Rodney's upper jawbone started growing. Maybe it had something to do with the kind of cancer.

I couldn't help but worry that the whole bone-marrow extraction procedure was taking too long. I mean, the doctor never really gave Rodney much of a break. But, to be fair, my sense of time was distorted, being that I was an observer during the whole excruciating ordeal. Dr. A. just kept drilling into my husband with that hideous instrument.

When will this end?

I could tell the pressure was getting to Rodney when Dr. A. suddenly said, "Hold on, we're almost there!"

Looking at Dr. A. about to give a few more twists, I panicked, realizing my husband was about to be put through unbearable pain. I leapt out of my chair, pushed Dr. A. out of the way, and went to my husband. While the needle was still sticking out of his hip, I slung his arm around my shoulder and hobbled to a nearby wheelchair.

"What are you doing?" Dr. A. shouted as I eased Rodney into the chair. "You can't leave now. I'm almost there!"

"I don't care," I said, looking back at him with a menacing stare. "Don't try to follow us. We don't need this stupid biopsy, because we're not going to do your dumb prescribed treatment anyway. Who cares if he's Stage III or Stage IV? I certainly don't!"

"Paige," Rodney said, his beautiful eyes reflecting his relief. "Thank you so much for saving me. Let's get out of here."

I slowly maneuvered him out of the room and down the corridor. "You got it!"

"That was so horrible," he groaned.

"I'm so sorry. I should have gotten you out of there much earlier."

The red-headed nurse followed us out of the exam room. "Come back! You can't just leave. No one ever leaves."

I ignored her, pushing Rodney down the hallway with every ounce of strength I could muster. As we picked up speed, the gown he wore flapped out the back of the wheelchair. The other patients, lining the hall, cheered us on. "It's a bird! It's a plane! It's Superman!" The roar of the ever-growing crowd was deafening. The patients regained energy as they watched us make our way down the corridor. "Look—they're escaping!"

"Maybe we can, too! Do you have any room for us on that thing?"

At that, everyone laughed. My husband had such an expression of pride as I raced down the hall, while the nurses all looked at one another in confusion. For a moment, I thought they might try to stop us, but when I shot them a glare, they all scurried away into various rooms.

Rodney's loud, heart-wrenching scream jolted me back to reality. *Ugh . . . I don't think I can handle this.*

"My body's on fire," Rodney cried out, his eyes glazed in shock. "Stop!" he cried. "I think I need more Novocain."

"Okay, I'll give you a little more." Dr. A. wiped his brow, injected him with more numbing agent, and then gave a few more twists! Dr. A. looked relieved and satisfied to have finally broken through my husband's bones of steel.

Dr. A. quickly pulled out three long strips of marrow and laid them on the tray. My eyes were fixed on Rodney, who still had the instrument in his hip. I was curious what the marrow looked like, but it felt like a betrayal to take my eyes off of my beloved. Barely breathing, I did my best to silently let him know that I was there and loved him.

"Okay, I need to pull the needle out now," Dr. A. said.

I flinched as Rodney did his best to suppress the pain while Dr. A. removed the needle from his bone. Although he didn't scream again, I could tell that he was in agony. I assumed that, since Rodney wasn't as surprised by the sensation, having just experienced it the worst, he was doing a better job of masking his pain.

Finally, the dreaded needle was out, and I could breathe again. Dr. A. was sweating profusely, his face a deep shade of red. Rodney's color slowly returned, but he still looked incredibly pale.

Dr. A. told him to get dressed, but when Rodney stood up, he got dizzy, sick to his stomach, and his face felt funny. He said his tongue was going numb as well as his left eye, and he was having trouble swallowing. When the doctor came back, he told us to wait there about twenty minutes for observation.

I mean, just watching it was one of the most difficult things I'd ever gone through, but living it? I just wanted to get him home so I could pamper him.

RODNEY

"I WISH I HADN'T ASKED FOR MORE NUMBING AGENT!" I said, slurring my words.

"You're so brave—I don't think I could've done that without being knocked out."

I smiled. She had a way of always making me feel like Superman.

Now that it was over, there was a dull pain in my hip, but I was proud that I had made it through the procedure. It was a rare kind of pain, one that most people would never need to experience, and I realized that I'd probably be able to summon the sensation upon command for the rest of my life.

It didn't take long for the side effects to wear off, so the nurse brought me a wheelchair. Paige and Brad helped me into it. It was good to have him there, as my wife would never have been able to get me into the wheelchair on her own. When we arrived at our house, I went straight to bed, falling asleep quickly.

Dr. A. called on Monday with the news that the bone marrow was clear of cancer. That meant I was definitely not a Stage IV but a Stage IIIB like we'd hoped. It was a huge relief, because it gave me a little more time and options.

I continued to reach out to friends and research on the Internet. An old friend named Drew, a six-foot-two African-American guy from Kansas City, said he had something to share with us but preferred to do it in person. He drove six hours in order to hand us a book entitled *One Answer to Cancer*, because it had helped his mother when she discovered a cyst in her breast. She had followed that book precisely, and Drew told me the cyst was gone within months.

Paige and I both read the book cover to cover and found that it made sense. The author, Dr. William D. Kelley, had cured himself and thousands of others with cancer by using a particular treatment method. He considered himself to be a teacher whose purpose was to educate people on the body, so that they could cure themselves of any illness.

Dr. Kelley stated that, "Cancer is basically a deficiency disease—a deficiency of the pancreatic enzymes." After my extensive study on the subject, that explanation made sense to me. I knew my diet was horrible. And, on top of that, I ran my own business, providing for a household with two children. Who had time to eat salads and focus on organic food? But if that's what it took to survive, I'd find the time.

What appealed to me about Dr. Kelley's protocol was that it addressed the entire body and lifestyle. It wasn't restricted to salve on lumps, or supplements, and didn't include outrageous practices like skin blistering. It stressed cleansing the body by stimulating the liver to do its job, which it can't do if it is clogged with toxins. Dr. Kelley stressed optimal nutrition, giving the cells what they need to run smoothly. Our bodies are designed to be well-tuned engines that purr along efficiently. Often it's what we put in them that plugs up the works. Farmers feed their animals better than we humans feed ourselves.

Thirty-three thousand patients had gone through Dr. Kelley's program, and about 90 percent had succeeded in eradicating themselves of cancer. I noticed that he didn't talk about lessening the tumors, like other medical professionals always did. No, he discussed how to completely eliminate the cancer in a body—once and for all.

This is what I've been looking for!

Dr. Kelley's program was almost like a foreign language. How many hard-working entrepreneurs gave any thought to the basics such as healthful food, clean, uncontaminated water, and adequate sleep? It just wasn't the norm.

The plan centered on a good diet. Fresh, raw foods with the addition of organ meats, like kidney, liver, and other ones I would have never considered ingesting. I was struck by a comment he made—that we eat too much dead food. And he warned that smoking, drinking, and any use of drugs were out of the question. Fortunately, that wasn't a problem for me.

I had no trouble seeing the connection between diet and health, once it was pointed out to me. In reality, I was malnourished. Of course, I took in plenty of calories with my fast-food diet of cheeseburgers, french fries, and other empty calories, but nutrients were sorely lacking. At 194 pounds, I looked healthy enough and had no clue that I was gradually starving to death.

Fifty years ago, it was thought that deficiency diseases didn't exist in this country, but today it is widely acknowledged that many of the major diseases plaguing much of the western world are degenerative diseases. These are contrasted with infectious diseases, which have external causes such as specific, identifiable microorganisms. Diseases originating internally, such as scurvy, rickets, and pellagra, have been understood since the early twentieth century to be caused by a lack of nutrients. The last half of that century saw an explosion of degenerative maladies such as diabetes, cardiovascular disease, and some cancers. All of these are best dealt with by prevention, which includes proper nutrition. But the Standard American Diet, which consists of food-like substances rather than real food, ensures that these diseases will only increase. Garbage in, garbage out.

Like a few other alternative holistic professionals I'd read about, Dr. Kelley also commented that the American Medical Association had little interest in curing disease. It was more profitable to let people get sick on the current food supply and bad habits and then generate billions of dollars in revenue *helping* them.

Dr. Kelley was run out of the country and persecuted for his offer to help mankind cure itself of illness, which, in my mind, was a very good sign that he was probably onto something. His book quickly moved to the top of my candidate list for treatment plans.

During his initial visit with us, Drew suggested we start juicing regularly. "Even if you don't choose this route, it will help you."

"Makes sense," I said.

"There's something else you'll learn about in this book, something I think you should also start immediately."

"What is it?"

"Your liver can't get rid of all the toxins that are building up," he said, "so it needs to detox."

"Uh, huh," I said, patiently waiting for him to continue.

"It's just that it's not a subject most people want to talk about," he finally blurted out.

Paige and I looked at each other. *What is he talking about?*

"Drew, at this point I'd consider eating live spiders if it would do the trick!" I said.

"Then how do you stand on the subject of enemas?" Drew asked, his voice low.

Okay, I wasn't expecting that.

"Uh, well, to be honest, I've never done one. But if doing them will improve my health, I'm in."

"Good!" Drew said, exhaling dramatically. He glanced at Paige, who nodded encouragingly. "Then you'll want to do the coffee enemas he prescribes in the book."

"Coffee enemas?" Paige and I asked in unison.

"I know it sounds weird, but coffee enemas help the liver get rid of its waste, allowing the bile to flow more freely. Once you're on the program, you'll do a Liver-Gall Bladder Flush, but for now, I'd recommend just starting with the enemas to clean things out a bit."

"In for a penny," I murmured.

"In for a pound of coffee," Paige chirped.

We all laughed.

Unfortunately, we soon discovered that there was a real stigma associated with the subject of enemas. After the third pharmacist gave us the same uncomfortable look when we asked for an enema bag, we hit upon the idea of searching on the Internet. We found it after a thorough search. Paige also found a website that sold coffee specifically for this kind of enema, which contained more caffeine and palmitic acid.

Who would've thought?

When the shipment arrived, Paige brewed the coffee per the instructions. It had to be boiled for five minutes and simmered for another fifteen minutes. It smelled like peanut butter as it cooked, and it was tempting to take a sip, but the bag was labeled "Not for Human Consumption," so we heeded the instructions. After the coffee cooled down, Paige handed a batch to me, and I couldn't help it—I just stared at the coffee, holding the enema bag in the other hand, wondering how the heck this was supposed to work.

You want me to put what, inside where?

In the end, Drew, being a true friend, told me exactly how to do it. I followed his instructions with difficulty, but managed. When I was finished, I was surprised that I actually felt better.

The coffee enema may have been first used in modern Western nations as a pain reliever. As the story goes, during World War I, nurses kept coffee pots on the stove all day long. Battle surgeons and others drank it to stay awake while working horrendously long hours. Enema bags hung around, as some patients needed help moving their bowels.

Pain medications were in short supply. Doctors were forced to save the pain drugs for surgical procedures, with little or none for follow-up after surgery. When surgical patients woke up from operations without the benefit of further morphine injections, they would scream in pain and agony from the surgery. They were also constipated from the anesthesia drugs.

As the story continues, one day a nurse was preparing an enema for constipation. Instead of fetching water for the enema, she accidentally dumped some cool coffee into the patient's enema bag, undid the release clamp, and into the patient it flowed. "I'm not in so much pain," the poor soldier said. The nurse took notice, and thus began the use of coffee enemas to help control pain.

Indeed, until about 1984, the coffee-enema procedure was listed in the famous *Merck Manual*, which is used as a handbook by physicians the world over.

When I came out of the bathroom an hour after I'd gone in, Paige was waiting for me with an odd, questioning expression. "How did it go?"

"Good. It's not easy, but I think I got it in the end," I said. We both laughed at the double entendre. Then I winked at her and said, "Okay, you're next!"

"No, thanks," she said, backing up, waving her hands in front of her as a protective mechanism. "I don't think so! I don't have cancer. I'll leave the enemas to you."

I chuckled. "It's not as bad as you think."

I let it go but planned to persuade her to try one later.

In the meantime, I continued to research. Although Dr. Kelley's approach looked good, I wanted to exhaust all my options. I found a number of impressive cancer clinics in Mexico. It wasn't practical for me, with my business thriving here in the States, but, for some, that would be the best solution. Some clinics were run by doctors who weren't allowed to practice in the U.S., due to their alternative-therapy approach.

Over the next few days or so, I received regular calls from Dr. A., asking if I was ready to start chemo yet. I continued to put him off, rather than give him a definitive "No." I didn't want to close the door on any treatment idea.

When my two-week period was up, I'd come to the conclusion that Dr. Kelley's treatment plan made the most sense and had the best track record. It seemed like something I could sink my teeth into, something I could believe in and pursue with confidence. Within his book were glowing testimonials from other patients who'd had Hodgkin's or Non-Hodgkin's Stage IIIB and were now cancer free. It was very encouraging.

Dr. Kelley's book told about a man who was a Stage IIIB like me, except that his situation was much worse. It wasn't just that his tumors were much larger than mine, but he'd started with traditional treatments, and the doctor had actually removed his spleen before giving him chemo and radiation.

When he realized he wasn't getting better, he switched to Dr. Kelley's protocol, sticking with the full program for three years. Years later, he was fully recovered, even to the point where he was able to have children. That's something of a miracle, considering that chemo usually makes people sterile.

Another patient, a Stage IV, started with chemo and radiation, and got extremely ill. He, too, switched to Dr. Kelley's treatment and improved. By the time the book was released, he'd been on the program for twenty-seven years and was still healthy.

The book went on to tell story after story of people who had conquered various types of cancer with Dr. Kelley's protocol. Patients from all around the world, all with different kinds of cancer, were responding to this treatment plan.

Now, I am only too aware that testimonials are not considered evidence and are anathema in the medical community. The "scientific method" consists of rigorous testing using double-blind placebo-controlled studies to establish the safety and effectiveness of their drugs. But, nowadays, most drug studies are performed by the pharmaceutical giants themselves rather than an unbiased third party. The FDA is too understaffed and underfunded to do the necessary tests for the countless new drugs that flood the market each year. The entire process is unbelievably difficult, due to the complexity of the human body, and healthy people are reluctant to ingest the powerful super-bombs being churned out these days.

Some studies are, of necessity, short and rather inconclusive, and the study has to be completed on actual patients. A good case in point is Vioxx. It was released before the long-term consequences were fully understood. It was known for years that the risks outweighed the benefits, yet it wasn't withdrawn from the market promptly, as it should have been. Profits came before safety.

So, when all is said and done, we have to trust someone or something. I didn't find any modality that didn't carry risks of one kind or another, and the benefits of a wholesome eating plan along with body cleansing made more sense to me than adding more toxins to my overwhelmed immune system. Since I'd already made up my mind, I sat down with Paige to share my thoughts. I looked her straight in the eye and said gently, "I think Dr. Kelley's program will give me the best chance."

She nodded, twisting the ends of her hair. "It does sound good."

I reached out and took her hand in mine. "But you're not completely convinced, are you?"

"I'll support you in whatever decision you make."

"Thank you," I said. "I can't tell you how much that means to me, but I really want to hear your thoughts. Your opinion is invaluable to me. What worries you?"

She paused and then let out a long sigh. "It just makes me nervous to go against the advice of medical experts. What if you just try chemo and see what happens?"

I couldn't help but grimace. "Paige, I'm not going to do chemo. Let's just say for a moment that I didn't lose two relatives to those drugs. Let's simply look at the evidence. Remember the book by Ralph Moss, *Questioning Chemotherapy*?"

"Yeah, I know," she said. "But this is different. We're not talking about abstract theories and data. You're my husband. I don't want to take any chances of losing you."

"I know. And believe me, I don't plan on going anywhere."

"It's just hard to ignore Dr. A.'s recommendation."

"Dr. A.'s only solution is chemo, which works by poisoning rapidly dividing cells. The problem is that it doesn't just kill cancer cells, it attacks anything moving. It's a Cyto-Robocop! It's toxic, and it suppresses the immune system. The death toll from that treatment just keeps increasing over time."

I paused, wondering if I needed to go on.

She put her hand up. "I can't argue with you on any of that."

"Dr. A. gave me a whopping five-to-ten years to live after chemo. At best! He doesn't even pretend to promise that his treatment plan will have any hope of actually curing me."

"I want you to be around a lot longer than five to ten years." Tears threatened to spill from her watery eyes.

"So, what do you think I should do?"

She shook her head. "I don't know. It's hard."

"I know it is."

"It's your decision," she said. "I'll back you up no matter which plan you choose."

"I know you will," I said with a grin. "We're going to have to do some radical diet shifts, though. I think you're going to have to learn to cook some new foods for me."

"That's going to be a huge challenge," she said. "However, how about I go on your diet with you?"

"Wow! Really?"

How did I ever come to deserve this wonderful wife?

She nodded. "It'll be easier all around."

I pulled her close to me and kissed the top of her head. I knew how hard this was on her, but I was sure that we'd get through this together, just taking it one step at a time.

CHAPTER 7

Russian Roulette

RODNEY

I WOKE UP THE NEXT SUNDAY MORNING FEELING DRAINED. Staying in bed all day sounded so good, but I realized that I would probably feel that way every day until I'd whipped my illness. Since hiding in bed wasn't what I wanted to do with my life, I forced myself up with the energy of an eighty-year-old and headed to the kitchen to greet the family.

Looking at my girls as they ate, I smiled. They were so young and lively, it energized me just watching them. "How about we go to the go-kart place later today?" I asked.

Jessika and Jade both looked up at me simultaneously with huge smiles on their faces.

"For real, Dad?" Jade asked. "I've never been on a go-kart!"

"I know," I said.

Paige looked at me questioningly, and I nodded with more enthusiasm than I felt. "Just give me about an hour, and I'll be ready to go."

Paige brewed me some tea, while I snuck off to do my coffee enema. Afterwards, I felt a bit better and focused on putting one foot in front of the other.

The day was a lot of fun. Fortunately, the place had grandstands for the parents, so I could sit and watch the girls go around in circles.

At one point, Jessika managed to get herself turned around, so she was facing oncoming traffic. It didn't matter, though; she and her sister had a blast.

When Monday came around, my two-week research period had come and gone. I knew Dr. A. would be expecting an answer, so when we walked into the office on Friday, we were ready for battle.

The red-haired nurse clearly wasn't pleased when I gave her my decision. Her face turned red, and she looked like she had just been slapped, hard.

"You shouldn't play doctor!" she accused.

"I'm not playing anything," I replied. "And if I were, I'd be taking on the role of patient."

She shook her head at me. "Rodney, you know you're going against doctor's orders."

"Yes. It's just that I feel I have the right to choose my own treatment."

"And die in the process?"

"Chemo has a really good shot at killing me before the cancer runs its course."

"It works well on a good number of people."

"And it doesn't work on even more," I said.

She opened her mouth to say something else and then quickly shut it again. My guess is that she probably realized it wasn't worth the effort. With an exaggerated shake of her head, she walked out, no doubt to tell Dr. A. how obstinate I was being.

Paige looked at me. "He's not going to like your decision."

"I know," I said, wiping my hands on my jeans.

"He's going to try to talk you out of it."

"Yup."

As we waited in silence, I went over the possible dialogue in my head. The only thing I was really worried about was that he might have the power and authority to *force* me to take the medication.

During my research, I'd run across plenty of stories from people whose doctors had pushed them to take chemo. One story in particular broke my heart.

A young boy in Florida had developed brain cancer. He underwent several rounds of chemotherapy but was getting worse. The hospital allowed his family to take him home. His parents decided to try alternative means to cure him and were having some measure of success. However, in the end, they were bullied by their doctors into bringing him back to receive more chemotherapy, which resulted in the little boy's death.

I wasn't a minor and knew that meant I should have the right to choose my treatment plan, but I still feared that someone might come knocking at my door in the middle of the night, demanding that I adhere to my doctor's orders.

Dr. A.'s cheerful greeting interrupted my musings. "How are you feeling today?"

I forced a smile, biting back the incessant waves of nausea. "Fine. And you?"

"I'm good. Thanks for asking." He glanced down at his charts. "Your blood work's improving slightly, and the white blood cell count is down."

Wow, that was fast!

He felt my lymph nodes and said, "Hmm, they feel a bit smaller."

"I've been taking better care of myself, eating right. No more snack cakes, junk food, and soda. I've been juicing vegetables and taking supplements. I've made radical changes in my diet. This was all quite a wake-up call."

"Rodney," he said with a frown, "drinking a little carrot juice isn't going to cure your cancer. You know that, right?"

"Yeah, I know, but it seems to be helping, right?"

"A bit, but not enough. We really need to get you on chemo treatment immediately."

I wonder if my children would understand the phrase "broken record."

"Yes, you've mentioned that," I said, "but I'm not ready."

"Rodney, you asked for two weeks, and I gave that to you," he said sternly. "The fact is that we passed that mark five days ago. It's time to start!"

It was tough not to take out all my anger and frustration on this man, but I knew that wouldn't help my cause. I glanced at Paige, who gave me a nod of support.

Turning back to Dr. A., I took a deep breath and said, "I haven't made up my mind yet. I need more time."

He looked back at his clipboard and flipped a few pages. "There's another option, one that might appeal to you more." He pulled out a brochure with a picture of a small bottle of clear liquid. "It's called Rituxan."

"Is it a toxic chemo drug?"

"No," he said with a smile. "It is classified as a monoclonal anti–cd20 chimeric antibody."

When I looked blankly at him, he continued.

"Basically, it's made from a single cell, which kills certain lymphocytes. 'Chimeric' means it was developed using another species' antibodies, in this case, mice. Anyway, it's a long-winded explanation, but it's not chemo."

"And the side effects?"

"All drugs have them."

I sighed. "Okay, but what are the ones associated with this drug, the one you want to put in my body?"

He flipped through the brochure and listed a number of typical and unpleasant side effects. When he came to the line that said that, in rare cases, Rituxan had been linked to a fatal brain virus, I stopped him in mid-sentence.

"No, thanks!"

"Oh, come on, Rodney!" he said. "It says 'in rare cases.' It doesn't happen often."

"Okay, let me ask you this then: How much does it cost?"

"About fifteen thousand," he said.

I nodded. "A year?" I began calculating what that would be a month.

"No, a shot."

"What?" Paige and I cried in unison.

"Doc," I said, "you know I can't afford that. I don't have insurance."

"We can work out a payment plan with you. Or, if you could get insurance, they'd cover it."

I stared at him for a moment, trying to figure out how long it would take me to pay it off, since insurance wasn't in the cards. "Let me do a bit more research, okay?"

"Rodney," he said, shaking his head, "you've done your research. You don't need to do more. Come on—it's time to get you treated already!"

"No," I said. "I'm sorry, Doc. I'm just not ready."

He flipped the pages back on his clipboard and sighed. "Okay, then. Just let me know when you want to be treated."

"Will do," I said, feeling like a great weight had been lifted from my chest.

He's going to let me go.

"Just promise me you won't go to one of those charlatans, okay? Those people who promise you the sun, moon, and stars, but give you no real proven treatment plan."

"I promise."

I guess I answered a little too quickly, because he gave me a heavy sigh and shook his head.

"No, I mean it, Rodney. I need you to take me seriously on this."

Fine, if he wanted to really get into it, I was game. "Then how do you explain some of the successes I hear about? People who have survived cancer and are alive decades later?"

"They're flukes," he said with a wave of his hand. "There have been a few rare cases of spontaneous remission, but no one knows why it happens, and it's impossible to trace. Maybe they hopped on one foot, or perhaps they ate Brussels sprouts every day for a year, or they might have just sat on the couch and watched TV. It doesn't matter; they just get better. Call it a miracle, but it isn't something you can figure out and do yourself."

I looked at Dr. A. as he spoke and could feel his sincerity. I wondered if some doctors might get major kickbacks for pushing these expensive drugs on patients, but I was certain that wasn't Dr. A.'s motivation. He really cared about the people he treated. Yet, I was disappointed that he wouldn't allow himself the opportunity to really study alternative approaches, like Dr. Kelley's. But I hoped that, maybe, through watching me get better, without taking the chemo drugs, it might change his mind.

Unfortunately, being realistic, I knew that he'd probably either consider it another fluke, or he'd lose his medical license if he ever subscribed to any treatment plan not approved by the FDA. He'd cure patients but lose his title.

Besides that, he'd open himself up to lawsuits. No one ever seemed to sue a doctor for injecting them with mustard gas, but if he were to suggest a change in diet along with pancreatic enzymes, he would face ridicule and ostracism from his peers—and possibly even jail time.

When he finished, I studied him for a moment. "I'm not saying 'No,' I'm just saying 'Not right now.'"

He let out an exasperated gust of air. "I guess I'll just put you on the watch-and-wait list then. Instead of seeing me once a week, come in once a month so I can continue to check on you. My door is always open if you change your mind. Just don't wait too long."

I was grateful that he was allowing me to leave and make my own choices, although it felt strange to feel gratitude for something that should be my natural right as a human being. Still, he could have made it harder on me.

During the ride home, Paige said, "I'm proud of you. You handled him well."

"He's a good doctor and a good guy," I said, closing my eyes. I tried to remember what it felt like not to be exhausted all the time. Oddly enough, that memory was fading, along with others. It was like I'd suddenly aged thirty years.

"I think I'd like him better if he didn't keep telling us that you're going to die," she said.

"Yeah, I know."

"Did I tell you about the dream I had last night?"

"I don't think so," I said. I couldn't be sure, though. I was usually pretty out of it and had trouble remembering even what I'd eaten for the previous meal.

"It was really strange," Paige said. "It was raining, hard. But instead of the rain being water, cancerous eyeballs were falling from the sky, all squishy and icky."

I opened my eyes and looked at her. "Okay, that's weird."

"You're telling me! I mean, this was not a light drizzle. They were pouring down from the sky and watching me from all angles!"

"Sorry, sweetie."

What was happening to my sweetheart? I felt responsible. Her life had been turned upside-down because of me and this stupid illness. Sometimes it's easier to be the one under the gun than the loved one standing by helplessly.

Paige tugged on her hair. "What's worse is that I think my hair is falling out in clumps. Maybe it's some sort of sympathetic reaction or something."

"Paige, that happens only with chemo."

"Yeah, I know. It's not exactly logical. Maybe I'm feeling sorry for all those patients in the waiting room. They looked really sick and weak, all slumped over in their chairs. Their skin is ashen, and their hair must be gone because so many are wearing hats or scarves. Anxiety is written all over their faces. They make me so depressed. It's so sad, like they're just waiting to die. I'm afraid people avoid them. Maybe it's the body odor chemo causes? I sense that they might crave attention and affection like anyone else does. I always try to make eye contact and give them a big smile and greet them when I come in. I think some of them really appreciate it."

"You're such a good, loving woman," I said, my eyes closing again of their own accord.

"Some are there with their spouses or children, but the ones who are there by themselves really bother me. I can't imagine having to go through what you're going through all alone. It just breaks my heart!"

"I agree," I said, wondering if my words were even coherent. I had closed my eyes and was drifting off to sleep. I knew that Paige would understand.

CHAPTER 8

Taking the Plunge

RODNEY

OVER THE NEXT WEEK, WE RESEARCHED DR. KELLEY and discovered that he had passed away just a few months prior. Paige diligently followed a lead, which put her in contact with his son, John. I was amazed that she'd actually managed to reach Dr. Kelley's son, and that put the wind back in my sails. I finally felt a little less like a marionette, where someone else was pulling my strings.

John recommended a nutritionist, Pamela, who had personally worked with his father, administering the protocol to many patients. According to John, most of the 33,000 people who had been cured by the protocol had something to do with Pamela.

"She's not easy to reach," he said.

"I'll get through," Paige assured him.

"It's just that she gets tons of calls every day and can't take them all."

"I can imagine. There are tons of people afflicted with various types of cancer. I read somewhere that one out of every three people get cancer."

"It's more like one out of two," he replied.

"Wow, that's horrible."

They hung up, and Paige gave me Pamela's phone number. I tried a few times, leaving messages, until, finally, Paige took over.

She called repeatedly, not giving up, and, of course, she got through, being that she's Paige and all.

I got on the phone and talked to Pamela for more than an hour. She had the voice of a radio announcer—soft, even, and smooth. I found it very reassuring and immediately liked and trusted her. I knew that I was on the right path.

I had various questions for her. Although there was a lot of information in Dr. Kelley's book *One Answer to Cancer*, there were a few things I didn't quite get.

"I've been taking enzymes from the health-food store," I said. "Can't I just keep using those?"

"No, they are not the type we use in our program."

"What makes yours different?"

"We extract enzymes from pigs in New Zealand. It's about thirty times more potent than the off-the-shelf pills at your local store, which use plant enzymes."

I continued to ask her detailed questions about the protocol. Everything she said made sense. The only thing that bothered me was that I couldn't talk to anyone who had gone through the program successfully.

"I've read a number of amazing testimonials in the book," I said. "It's just that I would like to talk to a live person and get their feedback."

"I do understand, but I just can't do it. All I can do is give you case studies without names, just like the book did."

"I understand the position you're in," I said, trying not to sound disappointed. "The bottom line is that I really like the program and think I'm ready to start."

"I don't know, Rodney," she said slowly. "It troubles me that your oncologist gave you less than 90 days to live."

"Yes, but I don't believe him," I said. "I think he's trying to scare me."

"Are you Stage IV?"

"No, IIIB," I said, "and, last time I went in, he said I was improving. He said it didn't really mean much, though, but I thought it was a good sign."

"What had you done to create the improvement?"

"I cut out all the garbage I was eating, for one thing."

"All?" she asked, drawing the word out for emphasis.

She knows.

I paused. Honesty would be important right from the start. I wasn't willing to fudge anything when it came to my health and my potential relationship with this nutritionist. She was holding my future in her hands.

"No, not all, but most of it," I said, "but since the other stuff is making me sick, it just doesn't go down well anymore. Overall, I don't feel like eating much."

"That makes sense," she said.

"So, what do you think?" I asked. "Can you help me?"

"As I said, I'm concerned that your doctor gave you such a poor prognosis. That's just not enough time for this protocol." Her voice became soft, with a touch of sadness. "I'm sorry, but I'm not sure this is the right course for you."

My heart skipped a beat. "I'll make it—just give me a chance."

"We have a waiting list, and we can take only so many people. I have to focus on the people who have the best chance of survival," she said. "Do you know that just a small percentage of those I try to help actually follow it to the letter?" she asked.

How sad. I was suddenly hit with the sorrow she must feel every day. Here she poured her life into helping people, and only a few actually followed through with the program. Reading over the book, I could tell that the protocol was stringent, but, faced with life or death, I would think anyone would give up cheeseburgers and ice cream. But then again, perhaps most people didn't have the willpower that it would require.

"I'll follow it exactly—I promise," I said.

"That's what they all say," Pamela said with a heavy sigh, "but they don't."

"I'm not like the others. I'll do it."

"It's more challenging than you think, Rodney," she said. "You're going to have to throw away a ton of stuff. You probably won't want to eat the things on the program. Not many do. That's why most quit after a month or two."

"That's not going to happen with me."

Pamela was quiet for a few moments and then said, "Okay, but Rodney, you said you plan to work throughout the protocol, not taking off any time. That's just not possible. No one does that. It's taxing on your system. You'll need rest."

I shook my head to emphasize the point, even though I knew Pamela couldn't see me. "I have to work. I can't afford the supplements otherwise. Look, you don't know how determined and dedicated I am, but I can do this. Let me prove it to you."

"If things get rough, and they will, do you promise that you'll quit working before you decide to quit the protocol?" she asked.

I thought for a moment. "I won't quit either." I was aware that I probably sounded a bit bullheaded, but I knew myself well enough to know that I could do both. I would work and do the program, with or without Pamela's help.

When Paige caught wind that she was still hesitant to take me, she picked up the other phone in the house. "Hi, this is Paige Stamps. I'm Rodney's wife."

That's my wife!

"I'll make sure he follows the program. I'll cook whatever is necessary for him, and I'll even do the program with him if that's what it takes."

"I can tell that you love him deeply, and that means a lot. The kind of support that you're willing to give is beautiful and not at all ordinary. In fact, I don't think I've ever heard of someone willing to go on the protocol with their spouse. It's very touching. It's just that he needs to be able to live long enough for the program to work. It takes some time for the enzymes to take effect."

"I know," Paige said. "It's just that he's not from the same gene pool as everyone else."

"What do you mean?"

"He doesn't smoke or drink. He's also someone who makes up his mind to do something and does it. I've seen determination in this man like you wouldn't believe. He has overcome a lot over the years. He's worked hard to get our business going, and, when things didn't work out for one business, he moved on. He never once considered anything a failure—just false starts. He's the most positive and motivated and tenacious person I ever met."

I cut in. "Something I don't always share with people is that I use visualization techniques. When I started getting night sweats, I would visualize a large, sharp sword. I'd shrink myself so small that I could enter my body with the sword and float on my red blood cells. And when I encountered a cancer cell, I'd slice it to death."

"That's great!" Pamela said with a chuckle. "Keep that up. A good, positive mental attitude is important."

"I will. And I'll do what it takes to get through the program as well."

In the end, she agreed to order a battery of tests, so that she could review the reports. She said she couldn't commit to taking me until the tests came back, but I took it as a good sign that she was moving forward as if she might.

At this point, I'll take any good news I can get!

I was surprised by the bevy of tests that Pamela ordered: Blood work, hair, and urine tests, just to name a few. She also interviewed me extensively on my typical daily meals and other health issues. Pamela seemed to require much more information than Dr. A. ever had. Medical doctors seemed fine with a hit-or-miss approach to cancer, despite their incredibly poor results.

As the days went by, Pamela continued to interview me, order more tests, and study my particular illness. After all was said and done, she agreed to take me, despite her concerns. Because I had a blood cancer, she felt that the enzymes would take effect more quickly.

Time would tell.

PAIGE

SINCE I TOLD PAMELA I WOULD FOLLOW THE PROTOCOL with Rodney, I decided it was time to get with the program. He was thrilled when I told him I was ready to try the coffee enema. So, that night, I made an extra batch of coffee, and, when I woke up, I went into the second bathroom. Looking at all the parts, I started to question my decision. But then, I just shrugged.

Just don't think about it too much.

I learned quickly to let the coffee go in slowly, by using the clamp on the tube. If it went in too fast, I couldn't hold it. Once it was in, I had to lie on my left side for five minutes, then on my back for five, and finally my right side for five, before I could get rid of it in the toilet.

When I came out, Rodney was there. He had a polite but inquisitive look on his face.

"So, how did it go?"

I wanted to be honest. "I hated it."

"It gets easier with time."

"I can see that it might."

"Do you feel the effects?"

"Not really," I said, "but I guess that happens over time as well."

"So, does that mean you'll try it again?"

I looked him square in the eye. "I'll do them every day that you do, if it makes you happy!"

"Wow," he said. "I don't know what I ever did to deserve you!"

"You married me," I said. "When I took those vows, I meant every word. I am your partner in life, no matter what."

He didn't say anything but nodded. It suddenly occurred to me that he was choking up, so no words were coming out.

That alone told me everything.

RODNEY

HOW DID I EVER WIN MY WONDERFUL WIFE? Although our meeting had been a little bumpy and our first date a little unusual, at least in Paige's eyes, it didn't take long for me to realize that this was the woman I wanted to marry.

I decided to propose on the three-month anniversary of the day we met. I had it all planned out. First, I picked Paige up so that I could take her to dinner. On the way to the restaurant, I stopped at my house. I went into the other room, brought out a little box, and handed it to her. She trembled as she opened the wrapping paper, her eyes glistening.

Everything was going as planned, just as I'd pictured it. But when she opened the small box, her eyes opened wide. She looked at me with a startled gaze. "There's nothing in here!"

"What? Oh, no," I said, looking into the box. Sure enough, it was empty. Horrified, I said, "That's not the right box!"

She glared at me, tapping her right foot. "This isn't funny, Rodney!"

I quickly retrieved the correct box and returned to the living room. Paige looked so cute when she was indignant, but now she softened her stance, with her head cocked to one side and a little grin creeping up on her face.

I walked over and bent down on one knee, just like they do in movies, and slowly opened the box. "Paige, I want to spend the rest of my life with you. Will you marry me?"

She gasped out loud and covered her mouth with her hands. Her eyes filled with tears as she looked down at the ring. She picked it up and finally said, "Yes!"

She threw herself into my arms, hugging me close; then she kissed me passionately. There was no doubt she wanted to be Mrs. Rodney Stamps.

PAIGE

ALL THROUGH DINNER, I COULDN'T STOP HOLDING MY HAND OUT in front of me, so I could gaze adoringly at the symbol of our love. How did he know my size? I couldn't believe it fit so perfectly. It was as if it had been designed to live on my hand forever. I knew that Rodney was my soul mate, and, from that point on, I never wanted to be without him.

We had been engaged only a few months, but everything just felt right. I leapt out of bed like a woman who had just downed ten cups of coffee, just too excited to lollygag. This was it—the day!

It was to be a small wedding with only a Justice of the Peace, me, and Rodney. We didn't have money at that time, so I'd purchased a tailored, calf-length angora dress, with pearls stitched on the bodice, off the rack. I curled my long blond hair and wore bold red lipstick, Rodney's favorite.

When I pulled into the courthouse parking lot, I saw Rodney strolling down the sidewalk. He had his hair in a tight, low ponytail down his back and was wearing a black tuxedo with a crisp white shirt. His red tie matched the single red rose boutonniere he'd pinned to his lapel.

He is so beautiful.

He walked over to me, holding his hand behind his back. As we got closer, he pulled his hand out to reveal a corsage of three red roses.

Happy tears threatened to spill down my face and ruin my makeup. I couldn't believe he had thought to surprise me with flowers on my wedding day. With all the fuss of trying to put our wedding together, the concept of purchasing flowers had totally slipped my mind. But Rodney knew a bride shouldn't get married without them.

As we strolled up the steps, I relished the beautiful sunny day. It was October, but you would have thought it was May. We took our seat in the hallway and patiently waited for our names to be called. It didn't take more than fifteen minutes before a petite lady's voice rang out. "Rodney Stamps!"

We jumped up and walked into the Justice of the Peace's office. Giant bookshelves lined the back wall, filled with large tomes. Dead center in the room was a heavy walnut desk with two ornate brown leather chairs. We pushed the chairs back a little and stood in front of his desk in anticipation of our ceremony. After looking over our wedding license, the judge rose. "Ready?" We both cried an enthusiastic "Yes," which made him smile.

As we faced each other, I gazed into Rodney's beautiful forest-green eyes, held his strong hands, and realized there was nowhere I'd rather be. For better or worse, in sickness and in health, and everything else that went with the title of "wife." As the judge prompted us to say our vows out loud, it felt as if the entire world had stopped spinning on its axis. The dawning of a new reality was here. We were getting married. We were going to get to spend the rest of our lives together, as one, instead of two.

Finally, the judge spoke the seven words that I had longed to hear ever since I saw Rodney standing on my front porch. "I now pronounce you husband and wife!" Rodney slid the wedding ring on my finger, and I slid a gold band on his. "You may now kiss your bride."

Rodney leaned over to me and gave me a tender kiss on the lips. When he pulled away, I looked into his eyes and then allowed my gaze to dip to his lips. I smiled, plucking a white Kleenex from the box on the edge of the judge's desk, and wiped the red smudge off my beloved's lips. I had officially marked my spot.

You're mine until the day I die.

Now, with our lives hanging in the balance, I realized those vows had more meaning than ever before.

In sickness and in health, my love. I meant it then, and I mean it now. I'm here for you.

And if taking coffee enemas right along with him made him happy, I'd do that, too. Over time, the enemas did get easier, and I started feeling better. In fact, I had to admit that they made me feel pretty incredible. I had so much more energy and felt an overall clean feeling that came from the inside, which is hard to describe. After a few weeks, I really began to like them.

I didn't think I had too much to detox, but since I lived in this modern world, with all its pollutants and chemicals, I'm sure my body had plenty of garbage to get rid of. It became a morning ritual for us both to enter the two bathrooms at the same time, each with our enema bags, and start our day with a good cleanse. It's hard for me to sit still, even for fifteen minutes, so I liked to listen to music, jamming out on the bathroom floor. While I listened to my music, Rodney said he focused on setting goals. He utilized every second to visualize how he could combat and beat his cancer.

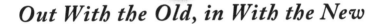

CHAPTER 9

Out With the Old, in With the New

RODNEY

PAMELA WARNED US THAT IT WOULD TAKE A WHILE to get the supplements, as the program had to be customized for each patient. So she had me start the program by doing the things I could, and I was eager to do everything immediately. Time wasn't my friend.

The fateful day that I called Drew to tell him I'd decided on Dr. Kelley's protocol was a real turning point.

Here goes. All or nothing. No looking back!

Drew made the six-hour drive again, and we all took a trip out to the health-food store so that he could pick out some pancreatic enzymes for me to start with. We also loaded up on other supplements and some good, organic food.

It helped that Drew worked in a health-food store and could guide us in our choices. We wanted to stock up on supplies, but Drew said, "No."

"At least, not on the food. Anything that won't rot in a few days needs to be tossed. The chemicals they use to preserve food, which give them a longer shelf life, are deadly for anybody, but especially for someone with cancer."

"Some things will naturally last a week or so, like sweet potatoes," Drew said, "but you're going to have to get used to food shopping more often."

Paige moaned softly. The store was a good thirty minutes away, and working sixteen-hour days made shopping downright difficult. But we'd manage somehow. We would find a way. We'd have to. There was nothing easy about this illness, but if there was a potential light at the end of the tunnel, it was worth any amount of trouble, expense, or inconvenience.

Drew chose some enzymes for me to start on, though he knew they wouldn't be the same ones I would get on the official protocol. I told him that Dr. A. was seeing improvement already based on the changes in diet and the coffee enemas.

"We threw out all the Teflon and aluminum in the house and use only stainless-steel pans now," Paige said.

"More people should do that, anyway," Drew said. "Aluminum leaches into the food, and Teflon's just evil. The big chemical companies are well aware of the links to cancer, but they still manufacture the stuff. It's crazy."

"Fortunately, we managed to find a rather inexpensive set of stainless-steel pans," Paige said. "They're great except that the handles heat up. The first time I grabbed one, I got a nasty burn on my hand."

"When we can afford better pans, we'll get them," I said to Paige.

"Until then, we'd better get some good potholders."

Paige related that she had a problem finding soaps and shampoos because she is horribly allergic to the perfumes and dyes in them, and now, we had the added issue that I couldn't stand a lot of smells. Also, hair sprays and gels were going to be a thing of the past.

I just smiled and called her my Wild Woman, giving Drew an exaggerated eye roll that made him laugh. I turned back to Paige apologetically.

"Sweetie, you are the most beautiful woman in the world and always will be to me. We're putting our marriage vows to the test here, and you're passing with flying colors."

"Aw," Drew said. "You two are amazing."

◆ ◆ ◆

Once Pamela agreed to accept me on the program, Paige went on a rampage, like a duck on a June bug. She cleaned our pantry and tossed everything that didn't rot within two or three days, anything canned or white. It was amazing what we'd been putting in our bodies before that. Some of the stuff had a shelf life of a year or two. What sort of preservatives must go into it to achieve such a feat?

I remember reading somewhere that a Twinkie could survive a surprising amount of abuse and still retain its shape, texture, and taste. One man subjected the tasty treat to extreme temperatures and dropped another from a twelve-story building. The Twinkie survived each time.

I found an article online about a teacher in Maine who was handed a Twinkie by a student. He started an experiment to see how long it would last, thinking it would be educational for his students. Little did he know that it would sit on his desk for thirty years, without rotting or molding. Bugs won't touch the thing.

I have to be honest. A few months before going on the protocol, I would have reached for something similar to alleviate my hunger, but that's probably part of the reason I got cancer in the first place. We've all gotten so used to convenience, wanting longevity for our food products instead of our lives.

The changes in food production had begun with the industrial revolution. The assembly-line method of building Ford automobiles worked so well that it was soon extended to manufacturers of various goods and even to the food industry. To promote longer shelf life, the parts of the food that went rancid were removed. Unfortunately, these also happened to be the parts that contained the most nutrients.

Gradually, there came to be fewer backyard gardens, and people got caught up in new ways of shopping and eating. Most had no idea that crucial nutrients were missing.

Frankly, I'd forgotten that food is actually supposed to nourish the body. The way I see it, if the animal kingdom wouldn't fight you for the stockpile in your pantry, you probably shouldn't ingest it. Sometimes animals have better judgment than humans.

In the end, our garbage cans were filled with flour, corn meal, chips, cookies, sugar, and all our other basic cooking staples. We bought a juicer and set up a schedule to visit the organic health-food store three times a week. From that moment on, we were determined to eat only organic produce.

There were countless challenges . . . to put it mildly. They were more like major obstacles, like climbing Mount Everest. One of the biggest hurdles was trying to down the organic raw liver. Pamela explained that it was vital for the program, because it contains important live enzymes and amino acids, but the stuff is so disgusting and slimy, it was hard to swallow.

In his book, Dr. Kelley pointed out that the modern diet is deficient in organ meats, which were once the cornerstone of nutrition for our early ancestors. There was a real concern that I'd get very anemic without meat.

Paige, being the inventive and creative partner that she is, immediately set out to discover a way to help me be able to stomach raw liver. She started by freezing it in two-tablespoon portion chunks, which sounded great in principle. I was eager to try one and pulled it from the baggie. Paige suggested that I could just chew it up quickly, and the flavor wouldn't come through.

It didn't work.

It retained its full flavor while being crunchy instead of slimy. It was just so terribly disgusting. I somehow managed to swallow the stuff and keep it down, feeling like a contestant on some reality TV show who had just swallowed a live beetle larva or a duck embryo. I was tempted to stick my tongue out to prove that it was gone but instead focused on not vomiting.

Paige looked at me intently. "How was that?" she asked.

"Great," I said with mock enthusiasm, fervently hoping that I wouldn't throw it back up all over the kitchen.

She looked skeptical. "Really?"

"Sure," I said with a toothy smile. "Hey, I have an idea—why don't you try it?"

Her expression of pure revulsion made me laugh. "No way!"

"Hey, I thought you said you were going to do this with me," I said, unable to let it go. "Where's your raw-liver popsicle?"

"Sorry. It's not going to happen."

"Oh, come on—it's not that bad."

"I love you, Rodney, with all my heart, but no way are you getting me to gulp down a piece of frozen raw liver. Nope. Uh, uh. No way." Each word was emphasized by a shake of her head. "However, I will continue to make them for you!"

I groaned. "Thank you, my darling, from the bottom of my stomach."

Since I was determined to follow the program, there was no way around eating raw liver. It was a problem we had to solve. Paige came up with the idea of blending it in with the vegetable juice. It sounded reasonable. The theory was that the vegetables would mask the horrendous liver flavor.

She threw carrots, spinach, an apple, and the thawed-out liver into the blender. When it was all liquefied, she poured it into a large glass. I stared at the brown goo and looked at her helplessly.

"Go on," she said, a little too enthusiastically.

"You've got to be kidding!" I said. "You're enjoying this a little too much."

"This one will be better," Paige said.

"And how do you know that?"

"Liver and spinach and apples are a nice combination," she said.

"When it's cooked!" I grumbled.

"Just try the drink. Come on—chug it!"

I sighed and downed the drink as quickly as I could. It wasn't completely liquefied, so I had to chew my liver smoothie in order to swallow it. It was still massively gross and disgusting. I looked up at her and smiled, knowing that strands of liver were dangling from my teeth.

I was immediately rewarded by her girlish scream, mixed with a cute giggle. "Rodney!"

"Yes, my darling," I said. "Would you like a kiss?"

She gave an involuntary shudder. "Not with half-masticated liver between your chompers."

I widened my grin and approached her with exaggerated enthusiasm. "Oh, come on! Kiss me!"

She backed up laughing, violently shaking her head. "No! Anything but that!"

I chased her around the kitchen for a minute before I rinsed out my mouth. The taste couldn't be tamed that easily, so I brushed my teeth with a mound of toothpaste for a few minutes.

Being a persistent caregiver, Paige tried something new the next day. She kept the liver frozen and blended it on high. Maybe it would somehow disappear into the drink that way, as ice might.

Nope, that didn't work, either.

Just after I finished the liver slushy, I tried to eat something to wipe out the flavor and nearly threw it all up. For some reason, it made the liver taste four times more potent. I learned to wait a few minutes before eating anything.

I don't know if I'll ever get used to this.

The next day, I came into the kitchen to find Paige with a determined look on her face. She never could accept failure and was adamant about finding a way to make this palatable for me.

"Figure it out?" I asked.

"I think so," she said, not looking up. "I have a theory." She dropped a frozen liver chunk into the blender with the veggie juice. She blended on high for a short burst. "If I blend it too long, it gets warm."

"And nasty," I muttered.

She pulled out a stainless-steel strainer and ran the juice through it into a glass. "See, no strands!" she said, smiling.

She was so proud of her new technique that I swallowed any choice words I might've had about the concoction. It was still brown but not so chunky.

She gave me an encouraging smile as I downed the glass. The taste was still horrible, but I didn't have to devote all my attention to keeping it from coming back up this time.

I'll take my victories where I can get them.

"Kiss?" I said.

She gave me a dubious look. "Rinse and spit first."

I chuckled and went to the kitchen sink to rinse out the taste. I went back to get my promised kiss, but she presented her right cheek.

"Sorry, you'll have to brush, with toothpaste, to plant one on my mouth," she said as I pecked her cheek.

"Thank you, Paige," I said seriously. "I know you put a lot into finding a workable solution for me. I do appreciate it."

"Anything for you, my Superman husband," she said.

I went to the bathroom to brush my teeth.

PAIGE

IT WAS HARD TO DISCARD OUR STASH of cookies and treats, especially for the kids and me, but I didn't want to tempt Rodney in any way. I have such a potent sweet tooth, but it was a no-brainer. The trade-off was too important. If all that junk remained, Rodney would be tempted to stray, and I couldn't live with myself if I knew my sweet tooth had endangered his life.

If Rodney had looked at me with his puppy-dog eyes, asking me for a chocolate cake, I would have refused, of course, but a part of me would have felt extremely guilty about not giving him what he wanted. However, if the cake mix wasn't in our pantry, it's not like I would ever run to the store just to cheat on the protocol.

Cooking for my husband proved to be even more of a challenge than I'd originally thought. Rodney's food had to be lightly steamed, not boiled, which didn't go over well with him. I was so limited in what I could use that the food always came out bland. I tried to be patient with him, but honestly, with all the things I had to do at work and home, I wasn't about to put up with his turning his nose up at the dinners I'd make.

I scoured the Internet for recipes, wanting to do the best I could to make the dishes palatable. I also purchased a vegan and gluten-free cookbook, in an attempt to try to prepare foods that Rodney might enjoy. One day, I found a soup recipe that sounded good. It took me forever to find the organic butternut squash it called for.

I tasted the finished soup and gave myself a pat on the back. I had to get creative, swapping out a few ingredients to make it protocol friendly, but, in the end, I thought it tasted pretty good. It was a major accomplishment for me.

He took one look at it and said, "This is horrendous!"

"You didn't even try it!" I glared at him. "If I'm going to go through all this trouble, the least you can to do is try it."

He closed his eyes and said, "You're right."

Staring at the yellow liquid, he took a spoonful and nearly spit it back out. With his mouth full, he looked up at me and immediately knew he needed to swallow it, along with any words of criticism.

"You need to eat. It's part of the program. Your body needs good nutrition to heal," I said gently. "I'll do my best, but you have to eat what I prepare."

He nodded and managed to swallow the entire bowl. I marked it as a "No" in my food journal, so I wouldn't make the same thing again.

It was all about trial and error. If one thing didn't fly, I needed to try something else until I discovered something that worked. I continually learned to improvise for his diet. Whenever he ate something, I would observe him carefully, all the while rewriting the recipe in my head, hoping to find a way to make it tastier for him. Rodney's determination to get well opened a door for him to try new foods, a door that had been tightly latched before.

As the weeks went by, my hair turned from blond to brown. Hair dyes and bleaches were a thing of the past, so I did my best to hide the new two-tone look. Looking through celebrity magazines, I noticed that various stars were sporting similar looks, something they called Ombré hair.

Somehow it looked much better on the starlets. However, it gave me hope that people might think I was hip and trendy, rather than lazy. Or perhaps they'd assume I was a free spirit, which wasn't far from the truth.

One of Rodney's favorite expressions was, "It is what it is." I always felt those were wise words, which seemed to apply to our lives more and more.

CHAPTER 10

Celebration Amid Desperation

RODNEY

OUR FIFTEENTH WEDDING ANNIVERSARY CAME IN OCTOBER. I didn't want to think about how this might be the last celebration for us, but the unwanted thought kept plaguing me. Since this was an important milestone, I wanted to do something to lighten our spirits. So I called a local florist and placed an order for a cheerful bouquet.

After I hung up, I leaned back in my chair, closed my eyes, and thought about our lives together. My entire existence had taken a 180-degree turn since Paige came into my life. I don't think about it a lot, because I live in the present and focus on the future, but I'm grateful for the happiness she has brought me. We have forged an unbreakable bond and a formidable team.

Right from the start, I knew Paige was the girl for me.

We met when I was twenty-three, with long hair, playing drums in a heavy-metal band. For years, I had been traveling with different bands, playing gigs all over the country.

When I wasn't traveling with the band, I was working different jobs, including working with my father in his electronics business, which involved installation and service of sound and fire alarm systems. We covered a lot of bases, and the hands-on experience taught me a lot. During those years I learned that high standards of performance with honesty, integrity, and hard work were crucial to success.

I wasn't exactly the guy Paige's parents had hoped she would marry. In fact, there weren't just a few naysayers. She came from a higher social echelon than I did. They were academics and professionals, while my family was more middle class. My being a musician probably was the most objectionable part. I might as well have been a drug dealer!

Our love was strong enough to weather all the storms that young newlyweds hit. In our case, we hit a hurricane, with various people in our lives bent on breaking us up. However, we soon figured out their game and just avoided them. As a result, our lives rapidly got better.

An opportunity came up for us to start a business in Oklahoma City installing coverings for gutters. The business was a newly patented idea, and that was the nearest available city where we could become a dealer for the manufacturer. Paige and I threw ourselves into the venture. She ran the company during the week, sending out mailers and setting up appointments for evenings and weekends, while I worked my day job in the security business. The girls were young, so Paige had them with her constantly. They would tag along with us when we did installations, hanging out in the truck and playing all day. Fortunately, they were well behaved, which made it possible to get our work done. The gutter-cover business was hard work, but we were used to that. We quickly got a reputation for being professional and efficient.

The winters were a little rough, because we had to chisel ice. I did most of the hard manual work, but certain aspects of the job required two sets of hands. Each panel was about five feet long, so it needed to be held in place by one person, while the other attached it to the side of the gutter and the roof. Paige would assist me, keeping an eagle eye on the truck, where our girls were playing. However, there were times when she could stay in the vehicle with the girls, coloring and playing games. They managed to have a lot of fun, and I have to credit Paige with being an inventive mom.

During the warmer months, we'd let the girls play outside nearby. Many of the customers were so entranced by Jessika and Jade that they would play with them in the yard. We received many recommendations and testimonials, mentioning how well we ran the business as a family.

Unfortunately, right when we hit our stride two years later, a larger company was given the product line in our territory and overwhelmed the market, making our small Mom-and-Pop operation unviable. It was hard not to be bitter, because we'd primed the well for them but weren't rewarded.

While attending a business meeting, a colleague made me an offer I couldn't resist. It required moving to Lenexa, Kansas, where I became district sales manager for a large corporation in the security industry. The work was challenging, and the pay was good, but I had a difficult boss giving me orders that didn't always make sense.

The grueling hours made me completely miserable most of the time. I was constantly on the road, covering branches in four states, and I felt like I lived in my car. Somehow we never really settled in and felt at home in Kansas. My family missed Oklahoma, and I missed my family.

In those days, it had always been a struggle to get home in time to put the girls to bed. I'd already missed much of their early childhood, and it killed me. Still, I did everything I could to spend a quality twenty minutes a night singing songs to them, reading books, and cuddling.

Looking back, I can't believe I had put up with that life for so long. I kept thinking that the whole thing didn't make much sense. I mean, if I was going to work seventy-hour weeks, I should put that energy toward my own business.

One night in 2003, I'd just had enough. Jessika, who was 12 years old at the time, hadn't wanted to let me go that night, and 8-year-old Jade kept saying how much she missed me. After I'd finally been able to drag myself away from them, I came into the living room and pulled Paige over to our sofa.

"What do you think about starting our own business?"

Her head swung up to me. "Could we move back to Oklahoma?"

"Sure—why not?" I would have preferred to stay in Kansas, but where we lived wasn't that important to me.

"Would we be able to work together?"

"Of course," I said. "That would be part of the idea. We could spend more time together."

"I'm in!"

"Now, it's important to me that you really think it over. We wouldn't have as much money to start."

"That's okay."

"And it takes a while to build a business. It will be hard work."

"I'd be with you," she said, climbing onto my lap. "That's all I ever wanted. These last few years have been miserable, with you gone and the girls at school all day. I hate it. I'd live in a tent if I could enjoy your company all day."

I laughed. "I think we can do better than a tent."

She thought for a moment. "You know, we could supplement our income in the beginning with a few odd jobs."

I gave her a squeeze. "That's a great idea. There's a ton of things we could do to earn a few bucks."

The next evening, I came home early and called a family meeting, so that we could discuss our plans with the girls and gauge their reaction. I didn't paint any pretty pictures for them but was brutally honest with how life might be in the beginning. Both Jessika and Jade convinced me that they would be willing to give up a few luxuries, if they could see their father more often.

We made the leap within a few months. That gave us a short runway to get our new business venture off the ground, because I needed to get certain licenses in order to start my own business. Also, Paige needed to get trained and certified in a few areas. However, we quickly discovered that most alarm companies were desperate for qualified installers. Paige and I cold-called around and were often hired on the spot.

The first six months were tight, so we opted to clean houses on the weekends for various builders. They needed their new homes spotless right after the construction crews were finished. It was hard, dirty work, and I breathed in a ton of toxic fumes from the chemical solvents, but we didn't starve and were able to get Stampsco off the ground.

Paige and I continued to work long hours each day, just as we had in the gutter-covering business. That business experience taught us some important lessons in business. It's much better to pour your effort and creativity into your own company enterprise, something you can control and build yourself. Still, looking back, we're thankful. It gave us the impetus to start Stampsco. It's more than a livelihood—it's our passion, to excel in our chosen field. No one can ever take Stampsco away from us. We still work long hours, and it is exhausting work, but it's our company.

This work ethic has stood me in good stead. I never let up, even when I was diagnosed with cancer, nor did I let up my entire time on the protocol, fighting for survival. As a result, we continued to expand each year, despite the economy. We simply focused on providing great customer service and producing trustworthy designs and impeccable installations. Eventually our efforts were rewarded.

I heard a door slam and was jolted out of my reverie. Jade came running into the room, home from school. "Happy anniversary, Daddy!" She raced to her room, with Jessika following close behind. Within moments, they returned with a wrapped present for each of us.

Paige handed me a card and said, "Happy Anniversary!" She sat very close to me, hugging me, not wanting to let go. I put my arm around her, feeling the same way.

I opened the girls' present next. They had found a figurine of two bears fishing, where you could add water to it and have it run down the small waterfall.

"It has a fish, Daddy," Jade said.

"I see that," I said, turning the gift around in my hand. It was cute.

"It wasn't easy to find, you know," Jessika said. "There aren't a lot of really nice figurines with fish on them."

"We went to six different stores," Jade said proudly.

"Wow," I said. "Thank you so much. I love it!"

They beamed, looking at each other and giving the other a light high-five. I glanced at Paige, who was still latched to me. "I guess it's your turn!"

I went to the hall closet and returned with a bouquet of multi-colored flowers and a balloon that said "Happy Anniversary" on it, along with a brown teddy bear.

"I just can't believe you found the time to get me gifts, what with your feeling so sick. You're just amazing!" she said, giving me a tight squeeze.

"Open our present, Momma!" Jessika shouted, handing her a package.

Paige opened it to find a little white dog with a purple bandana. When she pushed the button on its paw, it sang, "She's got Betty Davis eyes." Paige's eyes misted as she looked lovingly at it.

"This is the most beautiful gift I've ever received!" Paige said, giving them both a hug and kiss.

"You're welcome, Momma! We knew you'd like it," Jessika said.

"What's it saying?" Jade whispered to her sister. "I can't understand the words."

"It says she's got better days inside," Jessika whispered back.

Paige turned to her, confused. "What do you think it says?"

"She's got better days inside," Jessika repeated. "That's why we picked it out for you. You need better days inside."

Paige looked at me and then burst into laughter, with tears soon following.

I hugged her tight. "I promise you, we'll have many more anniversaries," I said. "I'm going to beat this thing."

Since Paige was on my right, Jessika came up to slip under my left arm. "I love you, Daddy." She wasn't crying—she rarely did—but she wouldn't budge from my side.

"I love you, too, Sweetie," I whispered, leaning over to kiss the top of her head.

Jade looked at us and said, "You need a third arm, Daddy."

She climbed onto my lap and hugged me. I had everything I could ever want right there.

CHAPTER 11

Keeping the Home Fires Burning

RODNEY

WE HAD BEEN HOME-SCHOOLING JESSIKA for that last half a year, because the school she'd been attending had toxic mold and mildew. Since she was home all day, she became a real help to her mom. Paige valued Jessika's presence and help enormously and insisted she couldn't have made it without her. Jessika became hyper-vigilant along with Paige, fearing that my lowered immunity might leave me susceptible to other ailments. Germs had no possibility of survival in our house with two stress-cleaners about.

In the mornings, Jessika helped Jade get breakfast and to the school bus, and they spent time together in the afternoons while we were working terribly long hours. Of course, we had friends of the family stop by, and we made them call us every hour to make sure they were okay.

No two daughters could be more different than ours. Though they are both fairly sensitive, red-headed Jessika is introverted and private, and Jade, our brunette, is outgoing, outspoken, and bubbly. We love having the variety of personalities in our household. There has never been a dull moment.

Soon after Jade learned that I was sick, she started having trouble at school. She'd call us midday a few times a week, pleading with us to come pick her up. I'd come by to get her and find a sullen daughter.

One night, after I had read her a book, I sat down on the edge of the bed and looked into her eyes. "What's going on?"

She shrugged. "I don't know."

"Your grades are falling, and you're calling us a lot."

"Yeah." She stared at her blue comforter, not wanting to look me in the eye.

"You used to like school."

"That was before," she mumbled.

"Before I got sick?"

"Yeah."

"Jade, can you look at me?" I asked, gently nudging her chin up. She looked up, and I saw tears threatening to spill from her eyes. "Talk to me. I want to help."

"If I go to school, you might die!" she cried, throwing herself into my arms. I just held her tight, as her small body convulsed with sobs. It was too much for any ten-year-old to face.

I didn't say anything for some time. I just let her pour out her fears to me until she calmed down. She had always been my happy-go-lucky daughter, and now she was miserable.

"I'm going to do everything in my power to get through this," I said.

"But, are you going to die?"

"I can't promise you that I won't, but I don't plan to. I want to live. I want to be there to see your children's children!"

"Can I be home-schooled, too?"

I shook my head. "You'd be completely bored. We can't leave you alone, and we have to be able to work. Plus, normally, you really do like your school, and you have a lot of friends there."

"But Jess stays home," she said, pulling back.

"Yes, she does, only because she can't go to a school with mold. Do you remember how her breathing was before?"

"Yeah . . . but it's not fair."

"None of this is fair," I said, giving her a squeeze, keeping my voice gentle. "But I promise you I'll do whatever I can to make things better. Okay?"

She didn't say anything but crawled under her covers and fell asleep within minutes. I sat there for a few moments, watching her. It was tempting to pull her out of school, but I knew it wouldn't work. She would need far more attention than we could provide, and there was no way that we could properly instruct her.

After a few more minutes, I tiptoed out of her room and closed the door. I found Paige in the living room and filled her in on the conversation I'd just had with Jade. "Poor girl," she said. "I feel so . . ." I paused, trying to find the right word, "guilty."

"You have nothing to feel guilty about."

"Logically, I know I don't, but I feel like this whole thing is ruining my little girl's life."

"She'll come around. Kids are resilient. She just needs a little time."

"I'll do something special with her this weekend—just the two of us."

"That's a great idea!"

"I just can't shake the feeling that I'm creating memories that might last for her entire life."

"You are," Paige said. "I am, too. We do every day that we live with our children. They remember the little things sometimes more than the big ones."

I nodded and lay back against the cushions, propping my feet up on Paige's lap and closing my eyes. As if on cue, our German Shepherd, Konan, came bounding up to me. I felt his cold nose against my cheek and couldn't help but chuckle.

I was so comfortable that I didn't open my eyes but continued to lie there and receive the attention from my dog. After he was done licking me, he lay down by the side of the sofa. My watchdog.

PAIGE

IT HAD BECOME A DAILY RITUAL for Rodney to come home and lie down on the couch at the end of each day. He enjoyed the spot in the center of the house, where all the action was. I'd get caught up on cleaning, while the girls would do their homework.

Our German Shepherd, Konan, liked to lie next to him on the floor, as Rodney recovered from the day's events. It was hard not to be jealous, as Konan had always been my dog. Watching him nuzzle my husband's cheek, I'd often think back to a time when Rodney hadn't even wanted a dog. He said it would be too much work and that he didn't want to shell out the money for a purebred. They aren't cheap.

I, however, was adamant and persistent in my request. Since Rodney worked long hours and the girls were in school all day, I wanted someone to keep me company. I scoured the *Kansas City Star* for a top-quality, purebred dog that wasn't too expensive. It wasn't easy, because I was extremely picky. I didn't want an American breed, but a German one. There was a huge difference, especially if you wanted to enter your dog in shows.

I found an ad that looked promising. When I called the owner, she confirmed that she still had three male puppies and said that I could meet the parents. You can tell a lot about a puppy by observing the temperament of the mother and father. As soon as I hung up the phone, I flew down the stairs and jumped in my truck to visit Rodney, who was working a corporate office job at the time. When I arrived, breathless, I waved the check for $250 that I'd just picked up from the bank in his face.

He looked amused and baffled at the same time. "What's that?"

"The money for our new puppy," I said. "Let's go!"

"Now? Where is it?"

"Rayville, Missouri."

"You're kidding, right?" he cried. "We can't just take off in the middle of a work day and go to Rayville. I don't even know where Rayville is!"

I beelined it over to his computer and looked it up. Pointing at the screen, I said, "Look, it's only a little more than an hour away."

He closed his eyes and sighed. "Sweetie, I can't go now, but tomorrow is Saturday. We can all go out there then."

"Deal!" I was so excited. I couldn't wait to meet my new puppy.

The next morning, I jumped onto Rodney as soon as I woke up. "Are you ready to get our new puppy?" He grunted at me, so I started giving him little kisses all over his face. He refused to open his eyes but was struggling to hold back a smile.

"Oh, come on, Paige. You just woke up. You can't possibly be ready to go."

I shook him a few times for good measure, sensing he might be drifting back to sleep. When he grunted again, I sprinted to the shower, calling, "Rise and shine. Our puppy awaits!"

The girls were much easier to rouse. I think they both wanted a new dog as much as I did. I had them dressed and ready to go on the living room sofa, while my dawdling husband took his sweet time. Finally, thirty minutes later, we were in the truck, heading out to the country.

When we pulled into the owner's driveway off a dirt road, I marveled at the five-acre property with rolling hills. I scanned the yard for the puppies but didn't see them. The moment Rodney put the truck into park, I opened the door and jogged to the front door.

Every man for themselves!

A friendly lady with chestnut hair opened the door. "You must be Paige!" She took us to the back, where the puppies were playing, all so active and rambunctious. One was especially playful, nipping at his brothers and sisters, wagging his tail with wild abandon.

"Let's get him!" Rodney said.

"No," I said, looking over all the puppies, "he'd be a little much. We need one that's a little calmer." I pointed out a quiet male who had excellent markings.

"How about that one?"

The lady shook her head. "Sorry, that one's going to my son."

Go figure! He's the pick of the litter.

Just then, another puppy caught my eye. He was lying down, allowing his siblings to hurdle him. "I want that one."

Rodney grimaced. "I don't know. He looks a little slow."

"He's just not as obnoxious as the others. Besides, I like his markings." I went over and picked up his chubby little body, admiring his huge paws, sweet breath, and ginormous ears. I figured he couldn't possibly grow into those ears, but the paws were a good sign he'd be a big dog.

I cuddled him, carrying him to the girls and Rodney. The girls loved him instantly, playing with him the moment I put him down. Studying him carefully, I was confident that I could show him.

"Are you sure this is the one?" Rodney whispered.

"Yes," I said. "Definitely!"

The mother and father were good sized, and their paperwork was all in order. I could tell he was going to be a beautiful, big dog. I named him "Konan." I don't know why, but that name just stuck out to me as perfect. Rodney thought "Bear" might be a good name, as he was all cuddly and cute, but I was adamant that his name should be "Konan."

We soon discovered that Konan had a strong instinct to hide. From my research, I knew that was a bad thing. Since it's important to socialize a dog quickly, I'd bring him out to play with the family every time he hid. It didn't take long for him to want to be with us, rather than holed up in another room.

I registered him with the American Kennel Club (AKC), hoping to enter him in shows. The name "Konan Stamps" had already been registered with the AKC, so we got creative and named him "Konan Von Par Stamps." Each male in his lineage had "Von" in their registered name, so we kept with that tradition. "Par" would stand for "Paige and Rodney" ("Rap" didn't sound as good).

Physically, he was perfect, but we quickly knew we had a problem. He'd bark and growl at pretty much anyone who wasn't in the family. I did my best to train him, but it became apparent that he thought of himself as the Alpha male. When he tried to nip the nurse at the vet's office, she suggested that we dominate him at home.

I had the girls take turns pinning Konan down. They would hold him down for a good five minutes every day until he understood his place in our family. It took about two weeks before he accepted Jessika and Jade as his superiors. Rodney, on the other hand, pinned him down once, and Konan immediately accepted him as boss.

Although Konan was great with our family, I couldn't take him out of the house without having him lunge at people. He'd bark and growl, his hair standing on end from the tip of his tail to the nape of his neck. He'd just try to attack everyone.

I took him to a police officer who had tons of experience with the K9 unit for the Overland Park Police Department. He had opened his own training school for dogs, so I went to his office and requested help to train Konan, hoping to break him of his aggression. Although you were expected to drop your dog off at the training facility for two weeks, I couldn't bear to leave Konan for that long, so I came back after a day to check on him. I approached the officer in charge.

"How's Konan doing?"

"It looks to me like he's already been trained," the man said.

I smiled. "I've taught him everything he knows."

"Then what's the problem?"

"I can't seem to get the aggressiveness out of him."

"To be honest, I'm not sure what the problem is. He's been great with us."

"Really?" I asked. "Because he always seems to be in attack mode!"

The officer looked puzzled. "He's been docile all day. Here, come take a look." When I came into the room, Konan didn't notice me at first. I watched him around the others and was surprised to see how tame he was. However, the second he saw me, everything changed. He went ballistic. Konan did everything he could to get to me as quickly as possible, barking and growling like mad every step of the way.

"Whoa! I see what you mean," the man said. "Well, the good news is that he isn't an aggressive dog—he's just protective."

"So, what do I do?" I asked.

"You can't break him of that. And really, you don't want to, because you want the protection. You want him to look out for you."

I took Konan home and continued to train him, teaching him tons of tricks. One of my favorite tricks was to have Konan play dead. I'd put out my finger like a gun and say, "Bang! Bang!" He'd roll over on his back, with his feet straight up in the air, his tongue hanging out listlessly. He knew I loved that trick, so he'd adopt that position if I ever got mad at him.

House training Konan was a dream. It didn't take long for him to realize the back door had chimes hanging on the door knob, so if he nudged the bells with his nose, we'd let him out. I'd never seen a dog do that before. He was just so smart.

Now, as I watched Konan lie on the floor next to Rodney, I realized my husband needed him more. And Konan knew that, too.

You traitorous dog!

"He loves your sweet face," I said, doing my best to hide my rampant jealousy. Rodney's eyes were closed, as he absently rubbed Konan's head.

"He's still your puppy."

I plopped myself down on the other end of the sofa. "Oh, I don't know. I think you're the new Alpha Male." I picked up Rodney's right foot and began rubbing it. He groaned in pleasure.

He deserved to be spoiled.

CHAPTER 12

Down but Not Out

PAIGE

KONAN AND I SHARED A COMMON GOAL, one we both took seriously: *Take care of our Alpha Male*. When I went to bed at night, I'd worry so much about everything that I never got a full night's rest. However, I felt a tremendous sense of relief that we at least had a battle plan to attack his cancer. And if it wasn't for our money problems, I might have been able to sleep a bit better.

One morning, I woke up with a bright idea. "I'm going to ask some of our bigger clients to help us with the medical bills. I mean, why not?"

"You're going to do what?" he asked.

I knew it sounded a little insane, but I didn't care. "I'm going to ask for a donation for your treatment. Someone out there should be able to help us cover the $800 a week that the enzymes will cost. There's just got to be some money out there for people like us."

"Baby, I don't think anyone's going to throw money at us."

I folded my arms across my chest. "I don't see why not. I mean, some of these companies donate millions to help find a cure for cancer. Why not save the life of one person. You!"

"It will be a long shot."

"It's worth a try."

"If anyone can do it, you can," he said, giving me a hug. "And, in the meantime, I'll work on increasing our income."

I went through the Stampsco contact database, looking for possible candidates. Scanning through the list, I spotted Mariner. They were a huge corporation that hired us regularly to do their installations. I had just read in the paper that they'd donated a large chunk of cash to a major cancer organization, so I figured they might be sympathetic to our cause.

I convinced Rodney to go down to the Mariner headquarters with me, so that we could try to get through to the general manager. Somehow, a phone call didn't seem right. As luck would have it, the man was in.

"Please wait in the conference room," the receptionist said.

So far, so good!

It didn't take long for the fit, middle-aged man to walk in the door with one of his employees, Sam. We'd worked with Sam directly on a few jobs and knew him pretty well. He was a bit of a recluse, a classic outcast, complete with long, silver hair that reminded me of Doc Brown from the movie *Back to the Future*. His yellow teeth and nerdy square glasses probably put some people off, but Rodney and I had always made it a point of being nice to him.

Maybe our good deeds will be rewarded.

The general manager looked puzzled by our presence, which was understandable, since we hadn't scheduled a meeting with him. I gave him a sunny smile. "Thank you for meeting with us on such short notice."

He nodded. "What can I do for you? Is there a problem with the high rise?" he asked, referring to our current project with them.

"No, not at all," Rodney said. "Everything's on schedule."

"That's good to hear."

An awkward silence threatened to envelop the room, so I turned to Rodney. He gave me a slight nod, and I cleared my throat. "Sir,

I wanted to ask if Mariner might be willing to help us out." I then proceeded to lay out Rodney's cancer story in a rushed tumble of words. I tried to stay on point, while infusing emotion into the story.

As I spoke, I watched the man's expression, hoping to see some sign of sympathy. There was none. He was completely unaffected by the news that my husband had a life-threatening illness. He didn't interrupt me but glanced at his watch occasionally with a bored expression.

I looked at Sam now and then, in an effort to include him in the conversation, but kept my eyes focused on the man who could potentially fund our treatment with Pamela. "So, if you could help us out, we'd really be appreciative."

As I waited for him to respond, I fully understood the expression "so quiet you could hear a pin drop." Every sound in the room was amplified—the air conditioner, the copy machines running just outside the door, the muted chatter of various employees, even the distant rumble of the traffic outside.

When Rodney shifted in his chair, producing a deafening squeak, the general manager stood up. "We don't do that sort of thing. I'm sorry." He didn't waste any time walking out the door.

I opened my mouth, madly trying to find the words to change his mind. What could I say to make him care? As I watched him vanish around the corner, I realized it was a hopeless cause.

Speechless, I turned to Sam. He leaned in to me and whispered, "There's always hospice."

I gasped in shock. It was as if someone had poured a glass of cold water over my head. He gave me a creepy smile and turned to follow the general manager.

Tell me he didn't just say that?

"Paige," Rodney whispered, as he tugged on my arm.

I turned to face him. "Yeah?" I asked.

"Come on—let's go."

The next day, we found a small package on our doorstep. Inside were two shirts with the words "Beat Cancer" emblazoned across them. They had come from Mariner. My guess was that they probably got the shirts from the cancer foundation as a free gift for the huge donation they'd made.

Rodney shook his head and held the thing up to his chest. "I'd be swimming in this thing," he said. "Can you believe they sent an extra large?"

Pulling mine out of the bag, I saw it was also an extra large. I shook it out and wondered how many people could fit inside it. "How terribly thoughtful of Mariner."

The general manager also sent over a few plants. Not exactly what I was looking for, but I realized that maybe he didn't have the heart of stone he appeared to have. Maybe he did care, just a little.

"I just don't understand why they couldn't have given us a small donation," I said.

Rodney sighed. "Actually, I can see how they would have to decline to help us. They can't just give money to everyone who asks, or they'd be inundated with requests."

"I suppose. And not everyone would be legitimate."

"Plus, I doubt they'd approve any sort of non-chemo treatment plan."

I didn't want to give up on the idea of getting assistance, though. While I'd had some of the wind knocked out of my sails, I wanted to explore other resources, like Jade's school. The next day, I called over and made an appointment with Jade's school counselor.

I explained the situation to her, and she was very sympathetic. "We always help out the school," I said. "We're very active parents whenever the fundraisers come around."

She nodded. "And we appreciate that!"

"Could we organize a fundraiser for Rodney?"

"I can't see why not, but I need to run it by the executive council. They meet in two days."

I left that meeting with a spring in my step. There was hope. I waited for the counselor to call back, positive something good would come of it.

True to her word, she called two days later. "I'm sorry, Mrs. Stamps," she said. "There's a policy against raising money for a parent. If your children were sick, we could bend the rules, but our hands are tied."

What?

"But, it's a good cause! The kids might learn something, and they could know they helped to save the life of Jade's dad!"

"I'm sorry," she said. "Truly, I am. If it were up to me, I'd approve it, but I can't."

I hung up and realized we were on our own. No one was going to fund our treatment. It seemed grossly unfair, but as Rodney would say, it is what it is.

RODNEY

THE NEXT DAY PAIGE AND THE GIRLS PRESENTED ME with a couple of Superman shirts, telling me that they would help remind me of my true abilities and power. I treasured the shirts. Not everyone knew what was going on, but the ones who did smiled when they saw the large "S" on my shirt. It was the ultimate inside joke, one that gave me superhero strength throughout the day, reminding me of my family's love, faith, and dependence on my getting well.

I was determined to stay positive mentally, but I was worried about our finances. Although the enzyme treatment cost far less than chemo, it was still more than we could afford. Pamela let us know that one bottle of enzymes would run $200 and would last for a day and a half. It became very clear that I would not only have to keep my business going, but I'd need to double our current income.

I needed to find new clients in order for Stampsco to expand. We had a real niche in the industry, so every time I picked up the phone to cold-call, I'd usually get some business. It was a matter of finding the time and energy to do the work required.

One client sent me a referral for a huge project with a large local corporation, who was gearing up to upgrade all their facilities statewide. I met them at their Oklahoma City office and scheduled a walkthrough at their second facility in Ada. When the time for that meeting came around, I was flat on my back, unable to move a muscle. Some days were just like that.

So, I sent Tony, who was super stressed at the time, because he had to pick up the slack. But it was the only way. If I was going to expand the business, I needed him to become less of a techie and more of a manager. He was used to having me be there, being the boss and working alongside him, but now he was thrust into a new world, dealing with general contractors and such.

Tony called me later that evening. "The walkthrough went well. I think we'll get the job." He sounded tired and more than a bit grumpy.

"Good! And the school project?" I asked.

"The general contractor's telling me I have to be in and out of the wing very quickly. Meanwhile, I have to be in two places at once." The words continued to tumble out of his mouth as he told me all the troubles he was having.

"Hey, I'm sorry, Tony. I know this isn't easy. It's not exactly what you signed up for. Still, on the plus side, you'll learn a lot."

"I'm catching on pretty quick, but it's a lot," he said with a sigh.

"I know you're being thrown into it kind of fast."

"You're sick and all. It's not your fault."

"No, but I get it," I said.

"It's okay. It's forcing me to man up, take the bull by the horns," he said. "Look, I'll coordinate with the GC, and we'll get it done."

"Tony, how do you eat an elephant?" He was silent for a moment.

"I have no earthly idea."

"One bite at a time."

He laughed and said, "Yeah, that sounds about right."

"And know that you have the sincere appreciation of Paige and me," I said. "I mean that. I really don't know what I would do without you!"

Our main work came from subcontracting for larger alarm companies and helping them with the installation on their big contracts.

One day, I'll be the one hiring out for the dirty jobs!

One of the largest alarm-installation companies in Oklahoma City was owned by a rugged mountain-man type named Peter. He sported a large beard and always dressed in a suit or collared shirts.

Peter asked me to meet with a client of his, a pool company with a new facility, needing lots of cameras. He wanted to show off their installation crew, Stampsco.

Coming directly from another job, I was wearing my Superman shirt. It was what I wore pretty much every day. It reminded me that I could succeed.

When Paige and I walked in, Peter scowled at me. I could tell immediately that he was upset, but I had no idea why.

"What were you thinking?" he demanded after the meeting.

"What's wrong?" I asked.

He gestured at my shirt. "What's that?"

I looked down and closed my eyes. "It's my Superman shirt."

"Why are you wearing that to a meeting with an important client?"

Who cares what I wear? I'm the installer.

I swallowed my anger and realized I needed to tackle this head-on with him. It was time to have the conversation. I glanced at Paige, who gave me a reassuring nod. "Have a seat, Peter."

I proceeded to tell him my cancer story and how the girls had given me this shirt to remind me that I could survive. I ended by saying, "Hey look, I'm sorry. I wasn't thinking, and I can understand why you're upset."

He held up his hand. "No, it's okay. I just had no idea."

"I haven't told many people yet, but I'm going to have to soon."

"That won't be fun."

"No, but I don't think I can get around it."

He thought for a moment and then said, "What if I hired you?"

Paige and I glanced at each other, as my heart dropped into my stomach. "I thought you were hiring me for this job." Was he having second thoughts about hiring me for this installation? I was counting on the income. Without it, I couldn't buy the next set of enzymes. "I'm up to the task—don't worry. I plan to work right through the treatment."

I might be dead tired, but I can still move this body up and down ladders.

He shook his head. "No, you can have this job, but how are you going to be able to afford the cancer treatment on your own dime without insurance?"

"I'll manage," I said.

"I know how expensive it is."

"Stampsco is expanding, and this is a thriving industry. We just need to secure more clients and keep moving forward. One foot in front of the other."

He nodded slowly. "Rodney, I admire your spirit and attitude, but if you shut down Stampsco and came to work for me, I could put you under my health insurance plan. You'd be covered."

I wasn't expecting him to say that. I'll admit that I was completely caught off guard by his offer. I looked over at Paige and noticed she was intrigued. "Wow, Peter. I don't know what to say. We'll give that serious consideration. Thank you!"

On the drive home, I couldn't stop thinking about Peter's offer. It would be a complete 180 from what I had planned, from what I really wanted, but it was a solution for the tremendous financial strain our family would need to endure.

When I got home, I went straight to the bathroom to do a coffee enema. I was used to them by now and found the experience to be peaceful. I imagined the toxins leaving my body as I lay there.

Afterwards, I cleaned up, showered, and went into the living room. Paige had dinner ready for me. I scarfed down the Alaskan salmon, organic sweet potatoes, and green beans. I found my taste buds were coming alive ever since I dropped the fast-food garbage from my diet. The flavors of the foods were coming out more each day.

"What did you think of Peter's idea?" I asked, as I helped her clean up the dinner dishes.

"It would mean giving up Stampsco," she said.

"I know, but all the bills would be paid."

"That's definitely a plus, but I doubt they'd cover the enzyme treatment."

I shook my head. "No, I'm pretty sure alternative treatments wouldn't be on the menu."

"Then what would be the plan?"

"Chemo."

"But you don't want to do chemo."

"I know, but can we really afford to do this all on our own?"

"Yes!" Paige said.

I smiled at her. She'd just voiced my precise line of reasoning, and I was relieved to hear it come from her mouth. This was too important a decision to make on my own, without consulting her.

I was so proud of Paige. She has always been my darling spitfire, ready to take on the world with whatever she had. Nothing seemed to intimidate her.

The next day, I told Peter that I wouldn't be taking his offer but thanked him for his kindness. He was one of the few people willing to stick his neck out to help me, and I appreciated that.

CHAPTER 13

The Protocol

RODNEY

THERE WAS A LOT THAT PAIGE AND I HAD TO DO to set up for the protocol. Dr. Kelley commented in his book that people rarely actually die from cancer. According to him, the waste products that the malignant tumors give off accumulate in the body, and that is what kills the subject. Without a way to detox, the body can't heal and rid itself of the cancer.

Pamela suggested that I begin detoxing as soon as possible, even before the enzymes arrived. So, I did a liver-gallbladder flush and continued with my coffee enemas every morning and evening.

Pamela also recommended that we build a near-infrared sauna, as a way to detoxify faster, and recommended me to an M.D. who specialized in near-infrared sauna treatment. You can't see near-infrared, because the wavelengths are longer than visible light. This sauna used incandescent heat lamps, which we could pick up at a normal hardware store. Rather than using high heat to sweat out the toxins, infrared heats from the inside, through the skin. I liked the idea of a cooler sauna.

I researched the specifications for the sauna online, before designing my own on paper. I chose a simple design, one that used plywood, electrical sockets and lamps.

Paige and I went to the hardware store and got the lamp bulbs, timers, switches, and the chicken wire. The chicken wire turned out to be hard to find, because not many people needed a small quantity of the stuff. The guy gave us a strange look, and I realized we looked very odd, me with my slight frame, and my wife with her two-toned hair, asking for a bunch of odd equipment and parts.

"What exactly are you making?" he asked.

When we told him about the project, he seemed relieved. The next day, we went with Tony to pick up a canvas tarp and wood at another store. Once we gathered everything together, he helped us unload the truck in our garage. I went over the design I'd put on paper with Tony, and we began to build the seven-foot-tall box. It was a challenge for me to lift the wood into place. It seemed like every five minutes, I was exhausted, and I hadn't done much. Even using the screw gun to fasten the walls together wore me out. I was grateful Tony was there, because I needed to take a lot of breaks.

Once we got the three walls up and the roof fastened in place, we screwed the light sockets into place. We positioned a stool in the center of the large box and installed one lamp on each side and three in the front. Then we placed the chicken wire over the lamps to prevent me from burning myself on the lights. Once we finished wiring everything up, I plugged in the cord, and the box lit up.

We placed the finishing touch on the box and added the canvas tarp as the entrance. This would allow the heat to stay inside the box and give me some privacy, as I would strip down to my underwear when using the sauna.

The whole procedure took some getting used to, but I could tell the sauna was helping. I put it into my schedule to sit for thirty minutes in the morning and evening, every day, putting my body as close to the lamps as I could.

Burn and die, you cancer cells!

I could swear that sometimes I felt the tumors moving, trying to get away from the heat, like worms tunneling through soil. I'd sweat like crazy and feel great right after.

Since I needed to juice on a regular basis throughout the day, and I needed to be out in the field a lot for work, I purchased a power converter that plugged into the cigarette lighter of my truck. It converts the 12 volts coming out of the cigarette lighter to the 120 we'd need to run the juicer. We'd stretch an extension cord to the tailgate and keep all the vegetables in an ice chest on the truck bed.

I was excited when the enzymes came in, a full two months after I was diagnosed. Pamela had me start with 20 and work up to the 72 I'd be taking throughout the program. With 50+ vitamins and other supplements, the cost was about $400 a week, but I was not deterred. I had everything else worked out and was eager to start.

This is it! This is going to work.

My protocol was pretty routine. I'd get up at six in the morning most days and check my urine to make sure it wasn't too acidic. If it was, I mixed a powder that balances pH levels in a glass of water and drank it. Then I'd have a cup of tea, switching between Chinese Green Tea, Essiac, and Pau de' Arco each week. Next came the 12 enzymes, 6 probiotics, and then the Zinc, Manganese, Magnesium, and Chromium drops. I had various other supplements to down before I took the Metal Free drops and hopped in the sauna for thirty minutes.

Metal Free was amazing. You just put a few drops in your mouth, go into the sauna, and it helps rid your body of unwanted metals. Sometimes the liquid would hit my back teeth, where my old fillings were, and would eat them out of my mouth!

It's strange that some dentists still use mercury fillings, even with all the studies out there proving they are poisonous. The white ones work just as well, and though they may cost a bit more, I don't think you can put a price on your health.

Then I'd have a selectrolyte drink after the sauna and head for the bathroom for the coffee enema. After that, I would take a warm shower with filtered water.

For breakfast, I had a very specific diet, which included a special cereal made from multiple grains. We had a local health-food store close to home, but sadly, it had very few items I needed, so we had to make the trek out to the bigger one, 45 minutes away, at least once a week. Although Paige offered to go alone, I liked to shop with her. She didn't want to be apart from me for any length of time, and I felt the same way.

The larger health-food store had only 10 of the 14 grains called for by the program, but Pamela said that would suffice. We'd also get most of our nuts, seeds, veggies, and fruits there. Later, we discovered that one of the major supermarkets near us had a surprisingly large amount of organic produce, which made things easier.

Paige and I were constantly reading up on organic foods. We subscribed to various magazines, joined online sites, and purchased dozens of books. Paige quickly developed a superhuman eidetic memory, retaining tons of knowledge, including nutritional information and recipes.

We quickly learned that not all organic foods are created equal. You had to watch where the produce came from, because not every country had the same standards for classifying produce as organic. Also, Pamela advised us to avoid any fish that came from a farm pond, as the mercury content was often very high.

All soy products were out, because it's an enzyme inhibitor. Since I was so deficient in enzymes, we had to be careful that nothing had even a trace of soy in it.

After I finished my cereal, I'd eat two soft-boiled or poached eggs, one slice of Ezekiel bread with organic butter, and ten raw almonds. Then I'd down twelve more enzymes and a number of supplements with plenty of water.

After breakfast, I'd head to my desk in the bedroom, where I'd work on getting all the design plans in order that I would need for the day in my business. I went through reams of paper, printing out all the specifications and requirements.

To save myself some time, I'd try to get all the plans created the night before, but it's a tricky thing, something not every company in town puts their mental muscle into. Many companies make a bad habit of breaking the basic safety rules on a consistent basis, so if an emergency happens, no one ever really knows if the fire alarm system will work. I'd say ninety percent of the systems out there aren't installed to code, which is scary.

Once I was done with collecting all the blueprints and paperwork for the day's jobs, I'd down a strawberry whey protein shake, which tasted much better than the liver smoothies.

If all went well, I'd be on the job site by eight AM, ready to install all the equipment. I'd then spend the day going up and down ladders, running wires along walls from floor to ceiling.

I did my best to have a glass of vegetable juice on the hour every hour, if possible. Paige would always have my lunch ready to go, out of the back of the truck. I'd have my calf liver vegetable juice with as much garlic as I could stand. She'd also pack a large salad and more veggies, along with ten almonds and tea. Then I'd take twelve more enzymes and other supplements. An hour later, I'd take twelve more enzymes and have another strawberry whey shake.

Paige and I would make sure to get home in time to eat dinner before three o'clock, because I needed to make sure to eat any meat before then. According to Dr. Kelley, the pancreas cannot digest meat after three in the afternoon because it stops processing protein. If meat is consumed after this deadline, the body can produce tumors. I wasn't about to take any chances.

I'd usually have another salad, along with the salmon. I'd also have my vegetable juice with liver and then swallow twelve more enzymes and various other supplements. An hour later, I'd have another whey shake with twelve more enzymes and, if I didn't have to go out again, I'd start working on the paperwork and any new designs for the next day. Plus, I'd need to update any changes in the blueprints that we found.

I would create my initial designs based on the drawings given, but they were rarely accurate. I quickly learned that, in this business, you can't wire a fire alarm solely based on the old drawings. It seemed clients moved walls and made other changes that never go onto any blueprint, so it was up to me to make those updates.

All my designs needed to be approved by the architects, engineers, and fire marshal. I also had to set up the customers in Quickbooks, invoice them, schedule future projects, and handle all of the accounting.

Before we went to bed, I'd take six more enzymes and a spleen glandular, and spend another thirty minutes in the sauna, followed by a filtered shower. Then Paige would count out the enzymes and supplements for the next day. She would also prepare the coffee for the enemas at night, so that I just needed to warm and grab it, without waiting for it to cool down the next day. We had a system that became a well-oiled machine.

My old schedule would never have worked. Before I had cancer, I would get five or six hours of sleep a night. It was always hard for me to go to bed before midnight.

Pamela told me early on that I must get at least eight hours of sleep every night in a pitch-black room.

"It has to be part of your schedule because it is an inseparable part of the protocol," she said.

"I could do that. But why's that important?"

"You need uninterrupted sleep, otherwise, things will disturb you in the middle of the night, and you'll wake up. The darkness helps in the production of melatonin, which enables you to pass through the four phases of sleep plus REM stages in accordance with your natural circadian rhythms."

Committed to the protocol, no matter how inconvenient, I followed her directions to the letter. I got rid of all the LED lights and put tight window shades up to block any outside light. When we were all done, it was amazing how dark it got when we closed the bedroom door. I swear we couldn't see two inches in front of our noses. And amazingly, I did get the best sleep that way.

PAIGE

I KEPT THE KITCHEN FREE OF TEMPTATIONS for Rodney, but we really craved sweets in the beginning—especially me, the sugar hound. Occasionally I would sneak the girls out to the mall for a frozen yogurt, but nothing more. The changes we all made were huge, especially Rodney, the meat lover. Ever since I had known him, "nary a vegetable crossed his lips." I went to great lengths to learn and develop tasty recipes and became quite imaginative, I must admit. To help alleviate our cravings, I developed a recipe for sweet-potato pie, which turned out amazingly. Since our taste buds were no longer blindsided by white sugar, they were coming alive. We could actually appreciate the taste of real food.

Jade wanted to encourage her dad to eat his vegetables, so she would create works of art out of the salad plates. The carrots were placed just so, and she'd make very intricate patterns to demonstrate her love. The girls followed the diet pretty accurately and were very supportive.

Rodney and I both developed food sensitivities. Oddly enough, we reacted to different foods. Pamela had warned us to watch for signs that we were developing allergies and was especially concerned that Rodney might be allergic to coffee. That would have been disastrous because the enemas were essential to the program. We were very relieved when we figured out that coffee wasn't a problem.

There were certain foods that made us both sick. I would react immediately, but Rodney's symptoms often didn't show up until two or three hours later. Sometimes I would cough like mad and feel horrible, so I made a diligent effort to keep careful records of what we ate. In the end, Rodney gave up almonds and two of the grains.

I talked to Monica on the phone regularly. Although she didn't like that we were going against traditional medicine, she wanted to know how Rodney and I were doing.

"You have to stay strong and healthy, Paige," she said. "Caregivers forget that. Sometimes they get sick, too, because no one is taking care of them."

"I could see how that could happen. I will. I promise."

"You sound tired."

"I am," I said.

"Are you getting eight hours of sleep?"

I laughed. "Yeah, right."

"But I thought you said you two were going to bed early, so that Rodney could try to get his eight hours."

"Yeah, we do. We even put up window shades and took out all the LED lights in the room."

"So, what's the problem? Why aren't you sleeping?"

I paused. "I pretty much just watch him sleep."

"You what?" she gasped.

"I sit there and watch him sleep. You know, watching his chest rise and fall."

"Doesn't he wake up with you staring at him like that?"

"I do my best to not stare," I said. "I look at him out of the corner of my eye. Sometimes I put my finger under his nose or my hand on his chest, but I do my best not to wake him up."

"He needs you to be rested, Paige! Did you know that, statistically, caregivers go way overboard and completely forget about their own health?"

"I didn't know that, but it makes sense."

That night, I did my best to fall asleep. I knew Monica was right and that Rodney needed me to be in top physical shape.

Then at about two in the morning, Rodney woke up screaming. "I don't feel well!" he cried. "I'm very sick!"

He was delirious and confused and tried to pull the covers off and get up. But I pulled him back into bed.

"You're going to be fine," I whispered. "I'm here. I'll take care of you."

"I don't feel well," he said, his voice softer, less panicked.

"You're dreaming," I told him. "Here, go back to sleep." I encouraged him to lie back as I rubbed his head and back until he calmed down.

It didn't take long for him to conk out again. It took me a little longer. Those outbursts shook me up, and I feared they might get worse.

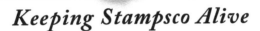

CHAPTER 14

Keeping Stampsco Alive

RODNEY

HAVE YOU EVER NOTICED HOW SOMETIMES bad things happen in a series of tidal waves rolling over you? That's what that period of time felt like for me—one massive tidal wave after another. I don't know what I would have done without Paige and my girls at my side.

I'd decided to take a stance against cancer, the Big C, and wasn't about to let anything stand in my way. But not everyone takes kindly to that kind of attitude. Not everyone appreciates a rebel. I think some people feel that you're being uppity when you dare to fight in a world where you're just supposed to lie down and take it. If the odds are stacked against you, you're deemed delusional if you think you might actually win.

Mariner, the big company that Paige approached for help, the one who flatly refused and then sent us a plant as some sort of consolation prize, called us in for a meeting about a week later.

Maybe they changed their minds. Maybe they found money for us!

Even being the optimist I was, I knew that was highly unlikely. This particular company had always been one of our more complicated customers. I guess that's par for the course with large corporations, where the right hand and left haven't always been properly introduced.

The different departments within Mariner were rarely in sync, often having no idea what the other was doing. And because of the way people have to claw their way up the ladder in such companies, the managers were always the smartest people in the room, if you know what I mean.

Way back when we started, Mariner was actually a decent company to work with, but when they took over another company, many of the faces changed. The first few projects after the merger went smoothly, but after that, the stress of the job probably kicked in, and their managers ran into trouble.

Someone lacking experience started underbidding projects in a desperate effort to look good. Then the design crew had to cut corners to make it all work. By the time they realized their error, they were stuck installing the fire-alarm equipment for an unworkable system. I think they were looking to us to bail them out, expecting us to make up the difference on the installation end. But our margins were tight, so we couldn't do much, which angered them. So, when they called to schedule a meeting, I wondered if that might be what the general manager wanted to discuss that day.

Walking into their spacious conference room, we sat at the table with the general manager, along with several other managers for the project we were hired to do. Paige sat on one side of me, while Tony, who met us there, sat on the other. Tony had also brought along a new hire, Sean, a young guy in his late twenties. This project would be his first job with us.

Our team felt small in their gigantic room, with the expensive, contemporary conference table between us and the executives. Mariner was our biggest client. They paid us six figures a year, and I needed that income in order to have a hope of paying for my treatment.

After the obligatory ten minutes of chitchat, the general manager finally said, "I know these projects must be rough for you with your illness."

Ah, so that's it.

Good—at least he was being honest. "Of course, it isn't easy, but I'll get the job done, just as I always have." I felt my heart hammering in my throat.

He studied me for a moment. "We just don't want to put too much pressure on you."

Like pulling your contract, forcing me to scramble for money wouldn't be putting pressure on me?

"Don't worry about that. Everything will continue as normal."

"Rodney, I don't know," the general manager said.

The other managers in the room were stone quiet. They obviously agreed with their boss, but again, that was the corporate survival mechanism at work.

I focused on my voice, making sure to speak slowly, so that my anger wouldn't show. "There really isn't anything to discuss here. We have a contract. Unless we don't fulfill our end of the agreement, you cannot legally terminate us without paying our fees."

"But what happens if . . . well, you know, things don't go as planned?" He paused for a moment and then added, "To be honest, you're not looking so good."

When I got over my shock at his lack of tact, I realized he had a point. Statistically, the chances of someone pulling out of an advanced stage of cancer were slim. I had dropped a ton of weight and probably looked like I was at death's door. And he wanted to know where his project would be if I died.

"I can always hire out," I said, leaning forward. "There are plenty of other subcontractors I could pull in, if I need to."

He looked me in the eye. "I didn't hire them. I hired you. We want you."

"Then I'll get it done," I said, leaning back. "But you can't pull the contract based on a what-if."

"It's a huge project. Maybe we can find a smaller project for you."

"What are you talking about?" I finally gave up any pretense of remaining calm. "I've done plenty of projects like this. You know that!"

"Not while battling cancer, you haven't."

"Just watch me."

"What if I don't want to?"

The discussion went round and round for another thirty minutes. It was only when the general manager saw that he wasn't getting anywhere that he finally relented and left the room. What else could he do?

The meeting made me realize I needed to keep on my toes when it came to all our dealings with Mariner, making sure to adhere to the letter of the contract. Any divergence would give them an excuse to terminate us.

"I can't believe that man!" Paige said on the way home.

"I understand his concerns. It's just his manner that leaves something to be desired."

"I guess it was a big mistake going to him for help. I'm sorry, Rodney. I never dreamed they'd try this."

"Don't worry about it. They're just sweating that I might not finish. It's just business."

"Sure, but did he have to go on and on about how he was just looking out for your best interests?" She lowered her voice to imitate the gravelly tone of the general manager. "Rodney, you're not looking very well. Maybe you should take some time off and rest, and let someone who doesn't have cancer finish this project." She did a fair impersonation of him, which made me laugh.

I adopted the same voice, although not quite as on target as Paige. "What if you die, Rodney? I know you need this contract for your treatment, but what if it doesn't work? Then where would I be?"

We both laughed, and I felt a little better. No matter what I ever have to face, I'm always grateful to have my best friend by my side. Paige knows how to cheer me up, no matter who tries to pull me down.

After that conference-room experience, I decided not to share the news of my illness with too many other people. It was tough, though, because word leaked out, and my noticeable weight loss didn't help. Sometimes a client would look at me askance and inquire, "Are you on a special diet or something?"

Yeah, I'm on the cancer diet, I'd think to myself. But in reality I'd just say, "Yeah, I'm on a very special diet."

They'd look puzzled, and I'd wonder if they had guessed. I'm sure some thought I was a marathon runner or something, while others probably assumed I had some sort of eating disorder. But both guesses were much better than the truth. Whatever they thought, though, I tried to lead them away from knowing that my doctor had given me only a few months to live.

After the meeting with Mariner, I realized I needed to make some changes within my business. If something happened and my cellular Samurais couldn't battle the defective cells, I needed a contingency plan for Paige and Tony to take over.

I started by breaking up everything I did with Stampsco into subcategories, so that I could write up detailed instructions for anyone taking over. I worked on it in my proverbial "free time," creating a huge manual that included each aspect of the business.

The technical side was challenging, but since Tony and Paige were well versed in that area, I wasn't worried about that aspect of the business. It was the administrative and sales end that concerned me. I needed to make sure they could handle closing clients, creating contracts, as well as billing and collections. In the end, the manual had twenty-six sections and was three hundred pages long.

I also began recruiting new employees, interviewing various technicians, people I could place in the field at a moment's notice to accommodate the increased workload. If I trained them now, Paige wouldn't have to worry about handling that if she had to take over Stampsco.

Another tidal wave hit when the life insurance company dropped me as soon as they found out I had cancer. You wouldn't think that was possible, and I'm sure it was illegal, but I wasn't able to fight that battle, alongside the one for my life, so I let it go. Yet, I felt an enormous weight from the added pressure of knowing that Paige and my girls would have no financial support if I died.

There were days when I was scared and overwhelmed, days when a black cloud of anxiety threatened to envelope me, squashing any energy I might have been able to muster. I did my best to ignore those feelings. What choice did I have? It was live or die. Giving up just wasn't an option. I had too many people relying on me to be that self-indulgent.

Time management became essential. I needed to do much more in much less time than I was used to. I did my best to stay at least two or three days ahead on scheduling.

With the threat of death looming over my head, I desperately wanted to spend time with my girls, but I had to stay focused on pushing myself to find new clients, invoice current ones, and approve design plans for all our projects. On top of that, I also had to make sure to get to bed early enough so that I could do my best to get eight hours of sleep each night, which didn't leave me much time for recreation.

CHAPTER 15

Could It Get Any Worse?

PAIGE

OUR PRECIOUS JADE WASN'T DOING TOO WELL. After Rodney had his talk with her, she had stopped calling from school. We'd get the occasional call, but I think she knew the strain it caused us to have to pick her up early, so, she just muddled through the day. Once a vibrant, talkative child, she was becoming more and more withdrawn at school. I longed for the days when she'd come home, telling us sheepishly that she got in trouble for talking to her classmates. Now, all we got were bad report cards.

One day, she came home with a note from the teacher.

Now what?

The handwriting was impeccable, a perfect copperplate script. My adrenaline spiked.

Although I wanted to know what was going on with my youngest, I dreaded the conversation. Ms. Tuttle was a college graduate from an Ivy League school, something we both respected, but she always looked at us like we weren't quite good enough to sit in her presence.

Rodney decided his Superman shirt wouldn't go over well, so he changed into a nice polo shirt and slacks. I changed into a dress and pulled my hair up.

When we arrived in the classroom, Rodney gave my hand a quick squeeze. Ms. Tuttle greeted us with a stiff smile. She indicated two student desks for us to sit in. I slipped right into mine, and, amazingly enough, with all his weight loss, my scrawny husband actually fit into his designated pint-sized chair.

Ms. Tuttle was impeccably groomed, as usual, and I noticed that her chestnut hair was swept up into a tight bun at the nape of her neck. From her tight, somber expression, it looked like it must be hurting her. I guessed that she might be in her mid-thirties, but her chronic frown lines aged her ten years.

She waited for us to settle in before she pulled up her adult-sized chair from around her desk to face us, putting her a good three inches above us.

"Thank you for coming in, Mr. and Mrs. Stamps." She engaged in some banal chitchat that I could barely stomach. Why do people feel the need to talk about trivial things before they drop bad news on you?

In actuality, it made us both feel a bit more awkward. We all knew there was an elephant in the room: An unpleasant, but inevitable, conversation about why our daughter was doing so poorly in school.

After a few minutes, she got to the point. "Jade is having some serious problems in school. She's failing a few classes and barely passing others."

Don't you know what we're going through?

"We know," I said. "It's just that her father has cancer, and we're struggling to keep everything together. It's been very difficult."

"I understand that you have cancer," Ms. Tuttle said, looking over at Rodney in a rather dismissive way.

Ah, so you do know.

"I am sorry about that," she continued, "but honestly, you must still work with your daughter. She needs your help to do well in school."

Rodney did his best to explain our situation. He managed to keep his anger in check, but I was having difficulty. It was hard to sit still when someone was basically saying, "Couldn't you just be better parents?"

She abruptly turned her attention to me. "How about you? Do you have time to spend with your daughter on her homework?"

I closed my eyes and did my best to absorb Rodney's mildness. It wouldn't do us any good to alienate this teacher. Jade was having enough problems without being labeled a problem child from a problem family.

I opened my eyes, planting a smile on my face that I hoped would pass as congenial. I went over how I was helping her on her homework, which subjects I felt might be areas in need of improvement, and then I asked her advice on helping Jade. I struggled to keep my voice calm and light.

She discussed various options for a while and then switched gears. Turning to Rodney, she said, "I am sorry that you have cancer."

"Uh, thank you," Rodney said, caught off guard. He looked at me as if to say, "I never know what to say to that."

She then proceeded to tell us all about how some distant relative on her mother's side had died from cancer a few years ago. The way she spoke, I could tell she considered herself knowledgeable on the subject.

"How's the chemotherapy going?"

Oh, no . . .

What was he going to say? Please don't go into our protocol, complete with the coffee enemas, with this woman who looks like she sorely needs one. I saw Rodney consider his options, and knew the instant before he opened his mouth that he was going to opt for the truth.

"I'm not doing chemo," he said quietly.

He might as well have told her that he was planning to jump off a bridge in the hope of bouncing the cancer out of his body. She looked horrified and had the gall to ask him what he was doing to treat his condition.

I stood up and glared at the woman. Jade would just have to get through this year somehow, but I wasn't going to sit still, watching this termagant drill my husband.

"That isn't any of your business," I spit out, seething. "You can question us about Jade's studies and home life. You can make suggestions on how we can help her with her grades, but you certainly may not criticize our private choices about medical treatment plans."

I could tell that Ms. Tuttle was unaccustomed to anyone questioning her on any subject, because she turned beet red and lost her voice. It was hard to tell if she was angry or embarrassed. My guess was both.

Carefully watching her, I continued in a more civil tone. "Thank you for your time. We will endeavor to set aside thirty minutes a day to do homework with Jade. I appreciate your bringing this to our attention."

She barely nodded, which I took as a cue to leave. Walking out the door, I didn't glance back but hoped Rodney was behind me. It was only when I got to the car that I turned around and vented on my poor husband. He knew me well enough to just nod.

Such a patient man.

When we got home, we talked to Jade. We wanted her to know that we were on her side. When she asked how the meeting went, we carefully schooled our expressions and avoided sharing the gruesome, sordid details. Her dad held her close.

RODNEY

"I realize that my illness is partly to blame for your struggles at school, sweetie. I haven't been able to help you as much, but I'm going to do my best to change that."

"You are?" I could feel the waves of her relief wash over me, as she looked up at me and smiled.

"I'll do my best to carve out some time, every day, to sit with you and help you with your homework. Of course, your mom will help you as well, but I want to be a part of it, too. It's fun!"

She gave me a big hug.

"Thanks, Daddy!"

Paige came into the room, sat down next to Jade, and asked, "Can I get in on this action?"

Noticing that we were all cuddling on the couch, Konan came over to join in. He stood in front of me, looking eager for a petting. I reached out my hand and obliged him.

Jade sneaked over to the other side of the room, where Konan's ball lay, and scooped it up. She held it behind her back and sat back down, with a glint in her eye. Konan was enjoying my attention and didn't notice Jade until I stopped. Then he sniffed around her, before going back to stand in front of me. He looked pointedly at me and then stared at Jade.

"He's tattling on you for taking his ball, Jade," Paige said with a grin.

"Looks like it," Jade giggled.

I didn't do anything for a moment—I just watched Konan. That didn't go over well, so Konan looked back at me and gave a low, playful growl. Then he proceeded to talk to me until I gave in.

"Who has your ball?" I asked.

Konan immediately stared at Jade, which made us all smile.

"Jade, I think you need to give him back his ball," I said with mock seriousness.

When she turned over the ball to him, Konan looked so very pleased with himself. Jade gave an exaggerated sigh. "I guess Konan is your favorite. You always give him what he wants."

I grinned. "He's so cute. How can I resist?"

"You don't think it's so cute when I tattle!"

I laughed. "Jade, you're cute no matter what you're doing."

She smiled and gave me a quick kiss before heading to her room. Paige watched her walk away and kept staring even after Jade had shut her bedroom door.

"She's okay, you know," I said.

"Yeah," she responded. "I just don't know how I missed that. I used to be on top of all her schoolwork. All the science-fair projects, you know—everything."

"Last year, I spent a full week with her on that project with ferns, testing soil and fertilizer. Remember?"

"Yeah, you two were thick as thieves, all huddled together at the dinner table," Paige said with a fond smile.

"Jade will forgive us. And next year, we'll wipe this year's memories away with all sorts of new, happier ones."

"You think?"

"I know it," I said. "As a matter of fact, I was thinking you and I should spend a bit of time and write down our mutual goals. We haven't done that for a while."

I went to get a notebook and pen, bringing them back to the couch. Although I really needed to get to the next day's design work, this was important. Writing down my goals has always helped me focus on them. I like to review them over and over to assess my progress. Plus, I felt more committed when I put pen to paper.

"Goal number one: Beat this stupid cancer!" I put three exclamation points at the end of the statement.

"Hear, hear!"

"I should clarify that. I want to be completely cured."

"Yeah," Paige said. "Let's do more than just find a treatment that might keep you alive for the next few years."

I put down the pad, leaned back into the cushions, and closed my eyes. "If I were cancer, I wouldn't have picked me to invade. These suckers picked the wrong host!"

"Yeah!" Paige said.

"They can't win, not without a fight." I grinned. "They can't kill Superman!"

"No one could argue with that!"

I opened my eyes. "Okay, that's the first goal. What's next?"

"We never did have a honeymoon," Paige said. "Being such workaholics, we never took the time to do that. I'm hoping we'll get a chance to go someplace, someday."

I nodded. "Good! Where?"

"Anywhere, really."

"Just the two of us, or the whole family?" I asked.

"The whole family."

I wrote down, "Number two: Schedule a family vacation."

"Where would you like to go?" Paige asked, looking over my shoulder as I wrote. I could feel her heart beating against my arm. It was wonderful to see her so excited.

I looked over at our small collection of DVDs, mostly Disney movies. "Wouldn't it be wonderful to take a week-long vacation to Orlando and see all the parks?"

Paige's eyes lit up. "Yeah! That would be amazing!"

"There are so many places to see there."

"We have to see Sea World, too. The girls would love it."

I modified the goal to be a week-long trip to Orlando.

"Okay, and for number three, I have one more goal."

"And that would be . . ."

"I want to buy a house. I'm tired of renting."

Her face scrunched up a bit. "Really?"

"Yeah, really!" I said. "Part of the point here is to stretch ourselves, go for something fun. I don't want to just not die. You know what I mean?"

"It's just, what's going to happen if things don't work out and I'm left with a mortgage?"

I shook my head. "That won't happen. Besides, I'm not saying let's buy a house right this very minute. We can't afford the down payment. But if we continue to work hard, we might be able to before too long. And within a few months, I should be in better shape. We can wait until I'm out of the woods."

She smiled and said, "Okay, go for it. Put it down."

"We've got to figure out the details, though. It's no good creating generic goals. So, what do you want our new home to have?"

"A huge backyard!" Paige said. "Konan and the girls need a place to run and play."

"Big enough for a swimming pool, too," I said, writing it down.

"At least three bedrooms and two baths."

I chuckled. "We want a good school district, too."

Once I had all the specifics down, I looked over our three goals. I could have written many more, but I wanted to focus on a manageable number. I intended for each to come true. These three were the ones I really wanted, the ones I couldn't give up on:

Beat cancer, go on a family vacation, and buy a house.

I can do these!

CHAPTER 16

What Doesn't Kill You . . .

RODNEY

OVER THE NEXT TWO MONTHS, I CHANNELED MY ATTEN-TION toward the three goals I had created with Paige. They gave me encouragement and strength when I felt like I couldn't take another step.

I stuck with the protocol, refusing to deviate from it even an inch. It was hard to believe that I had gotten so used to the coffee enemas. I would have never imagined they would become part of my daily ritual.

I swear, whenever I talk to people about the protocol, that's what they fixate on. It became such a popular subject for people that I started singing, "The best part of waking up, is coffee in your butt!"

It always got a laugh.

Actually, the best part of waking up was Konan. He was always an early riser, waking up before the alarm went off. There were some days when I wasn't eager to get out of the warm bed. One day in particular, I knew I had a mountain of work waiting for me and an unpleasant project manager from Mariner to contend with.

Just a few more minutes . . .

Konan was much better than any alarm clock. He walked up, standing next to my side of the bed, and let out a low growl. I heard him but chose to ignore the intrusive sound, hoping he'd go away.

He was doing his best not to wake up his mistress but wanted my attention more than anything. Since I wasn't responding, he increased his volume and intensity, carrying on until I relented. I allowed my hand to drop off the side of the bed, dangling.

Encouraged by the movement, Konan lifted my hand with his cold nose, to get me to pet him. At that point, what other choice did I have? I obliged. That entertained him for a good minute before he grew tired of his half-conscious master petting him with a rather lifeless hand.

"Hello," Konan said in his growly speech.

Paige had taught him that. You wouldn't think you could teach a dog to say words, but she did, somehow. Paige also taught him "Momma," which he could say correctly if prompted. It took quite a bit of concentration on his part, which was always accented by a sweep of his tail on the ground.

He kept this up until I opened my eyes.

Okay, I'm up!

"You're such a good dog! What an amazing dog you are, Konan!"

I swallowed my enzymes and supplements, drank my tea, sat in the sauna, took my coffee enema, and hopped into the shower. Now, it was time to face the day. I wasn't looking forward to opening up my email. Lately, I'd been getting rather nasty emails from one of the managers at Mariner.

What a nightmare! If I hadn't been so desperate for the money, I would have told them to go fly a kite a long time ago. Once I had the money I needed to survive, I vowed I'd never work with Mariner again.

As it stood now, their design team had worked up blueprints that would never work, because they weren't up to code. It became clear that they were well aware of the problem when I pointed it out, yet they responded with, "Install it the way we tell you."

I let the project manager know that I would do as he asked but that I'd need to let the local Fire Marshal know that the system wasn't compliant. I had that duty and obligation.

My response earned me many venomous looks and comments. Between that discussion and the general manager trying to fire me before I'd even started, I knew things weren't going to run smoothly.

Sure enough, sitting in my inbox were three emails, all demanding that I get my butt in gear (although he used much more colorful language) and finish the project. It made my adrenaline spike. I had no choice but to go out on site and help Tony.

He was under the gun and the focal point for abuse from the Mariner team, as well as the building representative, who was a six-foot-four brute. Heck, the man could have been a defensive lineman for the Sooners. But Tony never wavered. He persevered under tremendous pressure, undaunted. The tension was palpable, but he didn't wither. We were so proud of him.

When I got on site with Paige, we went right to work. Tony came up and let me know that the building rep had asked him to work on floors that weren't on the schedule for the day. Poor Tony looked completely overwhelmed.

"I got it," I said, feeling weak and a little dizzy. I gave my illness a mental shove and placed a hand on his shoulder. "Just go back to what you were doing, and I'll take care of it."

"Thanks!" Tony said, looking relieved.

I called the building rep and asked if we could meet to discuss the project. When he arrived, his permanent scowl told me it wasn't going to be a productive conversation.

"You're behind schedule," he grunted as way of a greeting.

"No, we're not. We're precisely on schedule."

"Not by my calculations."

"And what calculations are those?" I said, allowing a bit of sarcasm to drip into my voice.

He didn't seem to notice the dig. "According to Mariner, the eighth floor's the priority."

I don't have time to continue arguing with this oaf.

"Look, if you want us to stay on schedule, I need you to back off. It's only going to create delays if you order my men to stop what they're doing to start a new floor. It's out of sequence."

"Not according to your boss."

"I'm my boss."

He scoffed. "No, Mariner is."

"Mariner's not my boss," I said, calmly. "They're my client. There's a difference. They hired us to do the installation, because we know what we're doing. We know how to run this so there aren't delays. Just let us do our job, and we'll come in on time."

When he saw that I wasn't going to back down, he stomped out, calling over his shoulder, "You better!"

We stayed for another few hours and then left to go to another Mariner project, a high school where we were running control cabling for an Automatic Building Control System. Fortunately, that project was almost wrapped up.

PAIGE

WHEN RODNEY AND I ARRIVED AT THE JOBSITE, we began unloading our truck. There were several men on the site, each assigned to do various tasks. But at that moment, no one seemed to be working. They were all looking in our direction, just staring at me, as if they had never seen a woman before.

This is so ridiculous! What's their problem?

I stayed close to Rodney and avoided giving any of them eye contact. I think the painters were the worst of the lot on this particular site. They always seemed to act like wild dogs.

I can't say that I ever got used to their kind of behavior, but after a few years of being on construction sites, I was almost immune to it. I had the notion that, as long as I could prove myself to be a hard and competent worker, people would take notice and treat me like an equal. I guess that was a little naïve.

The general contractor for the project, a middle-aged, balding man with a potbelly, walked briskly over to us, his face crimson. He didn't look me in the eye but focused on Rodney instead. Leaning in, he whispered,

"You can't stay."

"Why not?" I asked, my tone demanding that he recognize my presence.

He finally turned to look at me, scanning me from head to foot. After giving me the once-over, his eyes settled on my right shoulder. "You shouldn't be here," he explained, as if stating the obvious.

"What?"

It wasn't like I was dressed in anything remotely provocative or that I was winking or flirting with the construction workers. I was wearing old blue jeans, a baggy T-shirt, and a hard hat that covered my hair, which was tied back in a low ponytail.

"You're a distraction," the general contractor said.

When I looked over at Rodney, his mouth was hanging open. We had never been denied access to a job site before. This was new territory for both of us.

It took a moment for Rodney to find his voice, but when he did, he blasted the guy.

"You've got to be kidding! Why don't you put your dogs on a leash and let us do our jobs."

He shook his head. "I'm sorry. I can't do that."

Rodney closed his eyes. It looked like he was counting to ten. When he opened them, he began again with a calmer voice. "Paige can outwork any man on your construction site."

"I'm sure she can," he said with an exaggerated sigh. To his credit, he looked like he wanted to crawl under a rock. "The problem is that no one here would get any work done if she stays."

"That isn't our problem," Rodney said.

The man then tried to explain how it would hurt Stampsco if the other men didn't work. He twisted it all around until he came out looking like the good guy, at least in his mind. He had it all beautifully rationalized.

Rodney and I didn't give up easily. We tried to reason with him from every angle, but he just continued to point out his idle men scattered around the yard. His argument was emphasized by the leering looks some of them sent my direction.

Give me a break!

You'd think that people would be here to work, but no one seemed to be afraid that they'd get fired for such outrageous behavior. And I guess they were right.

Sending them home was, of course, out of the question for this general contractor. No, instead Rodney and I had to leave. The guy said we could come back the next day when it wasn't so crowded or work after hours.

How nice of you!

Rodney finally dragged me by the arm off the site. I grunted loudly that they were all Neanderthals, got into the truck, and slammed the door. Here I was NICET Level II, a very prestigious certification given by the National Institute for Certification in Engineering Technologies. It meant I knew my stuff. I earned that! Not many women had that level of certification. Of course, Rodney was a Level IV, putting him leagues ahead of others in the field. Still, Level II was respectable for a man or a woman.

"That was so far from acceptable, I don't know what to say!" Rodney said when he closed his door.

"Maybe I should cut my hair so I'll look like a man," I said.

He chuckled loudly until he turned to me and saw my furious expression. He coughed dramatically to cover his mirth. "That's not possible."

I vented for a few minutes while he just kept telling me how beautiful I was and how it didn't really matter. He reminded me that we'd get the job done either way.

"We'll just go back when there are fewer people and get the job done."

As it turned out, though, the day was already mostly over for us, because Rodney needed to get back home. He couldn't eat certain foods past three o'clock, so we needed to start his afternoon protocol early.

RODNEY

BY THE TIME WE LEFT THE SITE, IT WAS TIME to head home for my coffee enema and enzymes. I pulled into the driveway and looked at the porch.

"Didn't you say the enzymes were arriving today?" I asked.

Paige looked confused. "Yeah, I tracked them on the computer earlier today. They were supposedly delivered."

We went into the house, and Paige called UPS, who confirmed that the package had arrived. Paige went over the importance of the contents, and they submitted a ticket to check to see what happened with the driver. She hung up and ran her hands through her hair.

"In the meantime, you're almost out," she said.

"What do you think happened?"

"Either their tracking is off, or someone stole your enzymes."

"That's crazy!"

"I know," she said.

Paige went around the neighborhood, asking people if they knew anything. There were a few leads that came back to one kid who had been apparently bragging about having stolen a package off our porch.

What kind of person steals enzymes from a cancer patient?

Paige tracked the kid down to his house and tried to talk some sense into him, but with no success. He wouldn't admit what he'd done, so she finally gave up. And there was no point talking to the absentee parents. They couldn't be bothered with mundane details like their son's criminal behavior.

"We could go to the police," Paige grumbled when she got home.

"It's not worth it," I said. "Besides, it would be hard to prove."

"Sometimes I feel like I'm Donkey in *Shrek*," she said. "You know, 'I'm a donkey on the edge! Look at my eye twitching!'"

I laughed. "Me, too."

Paige spent twenty minutes on the phone with UPS, explaining that I was a cancer patient and how we worked eighty hours a week to pay for the treatment. In the end, UPS agreed to replace the enzymes and ship them to us as fast as possible. It softened the blow a bit.

With Dr. Kelley's protocol, I was on the enzymes for twenty-five days and then off for five. However, since we could afford to pay for the enzymes in only one-week batches and I'd have to wait a week for the replacement package, I just took an early off-cycle. Pamela assured us that it would be okay. These things happen.

"We own a security company and just had a package stolen right off our porch," Paige grumbled. "Not good."

"I thought our neighborhood was safe, but fool me once!" There was no way that would happen again. We installed cameras all over the outside of the house the next day.

◆ ◆ ◆

A few days later, Jade came home very excited about a new school project. I was happy to see her engaged again.

"Ms. Tuttle asked us all to make balloon cars at home so that we can race them in class on Monday," she said.

"What's a balloon car?" Paige whispered to me.

"It's a car powered by a balloon," I whispered back.

"Come again?"

"You blow up a balloon and connect it to the car. Then, when you release it, the air rushes out of the balloon, propelling the car forward."

We had five days to deliver a working balloon car. There was no way I could help her, but Paige threw herself into the project. She did research online and found various videos showing how to make one. Her first attempt was way too wobbly to roll with any speed.

"Mom, I need to race this thing," Jade said, looking completely dejected. "Besides, it looks . . ."

"Ugly?" I offered.

Paige glared at me. "Don't worry about hurting my feelings or anything."

Jade put her hand on her mother's arm. "No, Mom. It's fine."

Paige smiled at her. "How about if we call Tony? He's good at stuff like this."

"Yeah!" Jade shouted.

Tony was perfect for the job. Not only was he the ultimate handyman, but he was a racecar fanatic. He was always coming in on top at the local autocross races.

Over the weekend, he spent hours helping Jade design a sleek, aerodynamic wooden car that sported red and yellow flames on each side. Jade did all the work herself, but it was like she had Mario Andretti giving her pointers.

"No one's going to have a car like this," Jade said.

In the end, Ms. Tuttle had trouble believing that Jade had built the car herself. She won hands down, every race, with a design that far outshone any other student. It looked like a professional balloon car, if there was such a thing.

When she came home, she told us how another boy complained that her car looked just like the kit cars sold at the store.

"Did you beat him in the race?" Paige asked.

"Yeah, I beat everyone."

"Sounds to me like a case of sour grapes," I said with a smile.

"Ms. Tuttle doesn't believe me, though," Jade said. "She said she'd like to see the receipts."

Paige, being the organized woman that she is, had kept all the paperwork and made copies, so Ms. Tuttle had to eat crow and admit that Jade had done a bang-up job.

Jade's spirits soared, and her confidence blossomed as she completed fifth grade with flying colors.

Score one for the Stamps!

CHAPTER 17

It's Darkest Just Before Dawn

RODNEY

AFTER TWO MONTHS ON THE PROTOCOL, we were all finally getting used to the lifestyle changes. However, I was a little worried. I still hadn't felt much of anything, so I wasn't sure the treatment was working. Perhaps it had something to do with the fact that I hadn't started with the full seventy-two enzymes at once but had eased into the program gradually. Still, I expected to see some dramatic changes within a week or two. However, Pamela assured me I was progressing normally.

I didn't have to wait much longer, though. When month three hit, I became sick to my stomach. I have always despised vomiting, so this period was especially grueling for me. On top of that, the tumors began to swell.

I immediately picked up the phone and called Pamela. "I think something has gone horribly wrong. The tumors on my neck, arms, and chest are all a lot bigger than they were last week!"

"Hey, that's good news!" She actually sounded excited.

"What do you mean?" I cried out. "How can this be a good thing?"

"Before the tumors can die, they have to get bigger."

"But that makes no sense."

"That's how cancer works," she said. "The cells infected with cancer release a chemical when attacked that makes them grow."

"So, what you're saying is that the enzymes and supplements are doing their job, because the cancer is being successfully attacked?"

"You got it!"

"It's scary," I said. "It seems really counterintuitive."

"I know, but trust me. This is good news. The treatment is working. Well done!"

"I do trust you. I'll keep on it, just like I have been, just like I promised you."

"Perfect," she said. "But, Rodney, you need to understand that it will get worse before it gets better."

"Great . . ."

"The tumors will probably continue to grow on the days you're on the program, and then they'll shrink some during the off days."

"Don't worry. I'm in it for the long haul."

"Good," she said, sounding relieved, "because I've had several patients give up on me when the tumors increased in size. So many freak out and quit."

"That must be frustrating for you."

"It kills me!"

Sure enough, when I stopped taking the enzymes for five days, the tumors decreased a little, and I felt like Superman. I had all kinds of energy and felt like I could run a marathon.

Pamela warned me not to be tempted to deviate from the protocol, even if I felt on top of the world. Her job couldn't be easy, with people threatening to quit depending on whether they felt better or worse.

When I could, I took the time to enjoy the off days. I actually felt a bit like the old Rodney again. One Sunday in February, we all went out to a nearby lake, as it was unseasonably warm. We took a walk, just enjoying each other's company. It was such a nice break from the reality that had become my daily life.

Sure enough, just as Pamela had predicted, a few days after I resumed taking the enzymes again, I was sick as a dog. Those were some of the worst days on the program, especially because I couldn't afford to take any time off from work. I figured I was either going to be cured or die trying.

Paige and the girls became a bit frightened when the tumors grew. Some days, it got so bad, it looked like my chest might explode. On those days, Paige sometimes questioned the treatment. The weight of the world was on my wife's shoulders, so I understood.

Paige and the girls were the only ones who knew how bad I felt. As far as the rest of the world was concerned, everything was fine. I did everything I could to hold it in, knowing everything would work out if I could just stay the course. The last thing I wanted was to attract a bunch of naysayers, who would just encourage me to quit.

Three days into the fourth month, we got a great lead on a new project from another security company. We needed the money so badly that Paige and I agreed to take any work that came our way, even though we were already overloaded.

The job was for a refrigeration company who asked us to look at their fire-detection system. The first thing we did was schedule a walk-through of the entire facility. I planned to keep it short and then bid on the project.

When we got to the site, the owner gave us a tour of the facility and then wanted us to see the walk-in freezers. Normally, this wouldn't be a problem, but I had no idea that the extreme temperatures would wreak havoc on my body. The second I walked into the enormous icebox, it was like I'd been zapped by Mr. Freeze's gun from *Batman*. I knew I was in trouble within three steps when I couldn't even lift my leg to walk.

The last thing I wanted to do was have the cancer conversation with this new prospective client. I looked at Paige, silently willing her to understand my predicament. Fortunately, she instantly responded.

Paige stood close to me in case I needed to lean on her, but I didn't want to give away my situation. "I'm so sorry," I said, struggling to get my body to work long enough to get out of the freezer, "I just realized I need to be somewhere. I'll get back to you as soon as I can with a complete estimate."

The client never seemed to pick up on the fact that anything was wrong. He thanked me for my time and left. When he was out of sight, I put my arm around Paige, allowing her to help me to the truck, slowly. I was relieved that no one seemed to notice us hobbling out.

Although I never considered quitting Dr. Kelley's protocol, there were days when I didn't want to swallow any more pills, because I knew they'd make me feel even worse. Plus, there were just so many of them that I had trouble getting them down. In those moments, I relied on my discipline, which wouldn't allow me to whine too much.

I'd been trained in martial arts when I was younger. I studied *GoJu* under the tutelage of Greg Cross and Lou Angel. *GoJu* is Japanese for "hard-soft style" and is one of the main traditional Okinawan styles of karate, featuring a combination of hard and soft techniques. The training was so demanding and exhausting at times, I thought I was literally going to die. There were times when I would come home bloodied and bruised after training and fighting, and would need a few days to heal and recuperate before going back for more. I guess you could say that I learned how to take a beating in those days.

Martial-arts training helped toughen me up, but most of my strength and discipline comes from my faith in the promises found in God's word the Bible.

◆ ◆ ◆

I maintained my monthly appointments with Dr. A. Every time we went in, he and his nurse kept trying to convince me to take chemo. I successfully put them off, month after month, telling them I wasn't quite ready yet. I was afraid that, if I flatly refused, it would force his hand, causing him to try to force me legally. In hindsight, I don't think he could have done that, but, at the time, I didn't want to take any chances.

It was tough to walk into his office with a full head of hair, when everyone else was bald. I hated standing out any more than I had to, so just before my April visit, I shaved my head.

By then, I was showing steady improvement. Dr. A couldn't wrap his wits around it. It was clear that I was getting better, but I hadn't taken any of his advice and had refused his treatment.

After chatting with me for a few minutes, he closed the door, giving me a serious look. "Rodney, can you answer me truthfully about something?"

"Sure, Doc," I said. "What is it?"

"Are you taking treatment from someone else, maybe a family member? Are you just messing with me?"

I shook my head. "No, I'm doing what I said I'd do. Juicing and taking care of my body. I'm taking the alternative route."

He discarded my words with a wave of his hand, as if they were trivial. "All that stuff you're doing wouldn't make any difference."

"But it is."

Doc, take those blinders off!

He ignored me. "Rodney, now, this is important. I'm concerned that you're taking Rituxan from a less-reliable source, like from across the border. People sometimes do that, but that Rituxan is no good. It can kill you!"

I nodded, keeping a straight face. "Yes, I'm well aware that Rituxan can kill you."

He missed my meaning. However, he nodded, satisfied that I wasn't bootlegging cancer drugs. "It's just that I know you don't have insurance and couldn't afford the treatment, so I wondered and worried."

"I appreciate that, Doc!"

"Having ruled that out, it looks like you might be one of those lucky people who experience a miraculous, spontaneous remission."

Yeah, along with the other 33,000 people on Dr. Kelley's program.

"Doc, can I ask you a question?"

"Sure."

"Are you a specialist in my type of cancer?"

"That's a fair question," he said. "No, I'm not."

"Don't get me wrong. You're a good doctor—and one who cares about your patients. But you seem to treat everyone as if they all have the same kind of cancer."

"You're right."

I think I had read every paper on Non-Hodgkin's Lymphoma I could get my hands on, and Dr. A. knew that. I handed him a report I'd brought with me, discussing treating Non-Hodgkin's Lymphoma only after the cancer transformed into a large B Cell type of Lymphoma, which is far more aggressive.

"Doc, we need to think outside the box."

He looked it over, and, when he noticed the doctor's name at the bottom of the study, his eyebrows went up slightly. "Anything this doctor says I'd take as gospel. He's definitely an expert."

"That's good to know."

He looked up at me with a smile. "You know, I'm beginning to think you probably know more about your cancer than I do."

"That should be the job of every cancer patient, I think. Everyone should do research."

"I couldn't agree more. It's a rather rare viewpoint, though."

I hopped down off the examination table. "Am I good to go?"

He nodded and walked me back up to the front. When we got to the reception area, he leaned in and whispered, "Like the new hairstyle."

I grinned. "Thanks."

Looking around at the people in the waiting room, I realized that Paige and I still stood out, despite my shaved head. We were just too upbeat and happy. I think some patients probably thought we were pharmaceutical salespeople, with our nice clothes and enthusiastic smiles. Still, I felt better not sporting a full head of hair.

Back when I was first going over my options, considering chemo, Paige had looked me in the eye and said, "If you do chemo, I'll shave my head, so you won't be the only one losing your hair."

I thought that was the sweetest thing. How many wives would do that? "That isn't necessary," I told her.

She nodded. "It is. I don't want you going through this alone."

I was about to tell her there was no way I'd allow it when both daughters piped in. "We'll shave our heads, too!"

It's amazing how children hear every word you say!

Oddly enough, though, Paige's hair began to fall out in clumps. She had become a vegetarian to keep up with me, so we thought it had something to do with the lack of protein in her diet, combined with the tremendous stress in our lives. She refused to eat meat because she didn't want to tempt me in any way to give up on the protocol. It's true, if she were to have a steak, I'm sure I would have smelled it on her, just like you can smell cigarettes on a smoker. On job sites, I could always tell if someone just had a Big Mac. I craved meat, but I also had discipline. I've heard people say that the minute they decided to go on a diet, they wanted everything forbidden. If they decided to give up sugar or diet soda, that is the thing they would kill to get their hands on. I felt almost that way about red meat. I thought about it, visualized it, smelled it, longed for it, and obsessed about it day and night. Just a hint of a smell or a picture on a billboard or TV nearly made me go mad with desire. Every rump I saw, no matter where or on what, was transformed into a thick, juicy steak. But I'm an all-or-nothing guy. When I make a commitment, I stick to it.

CHAPTER 18

Emerging From the Shadows

RODNEY

OUR FINANCES CONTINUED TO WEIGH HEAVILY on me as I relentlessly plowed through the enzyme protocol. Too much was riding on our success, and we had no safety nets to fall back on.

Buying enzymes in weekly batches made Paige nervous, because it didn't leave any buffer room, allowing for shipping errors, neighborhood thefts, or other, random events. Seeing her point of view, I became extra motivated to expand the business so that we could afford to buy the supplements in larger quantities.

Up to that point in time, we had been primarily hired by large fire and security companies to do subcontracting work on the jobs they didn't want to do—the tough and dirty jobs. They paid us well, but it was exhausting labor.

I was eager to start designing and installing our own systems, so that we could be hired by the clients directly. The moment we could do that, our pay would double, maybe even triple. There would be no middlemen to take their share of the money. The tricky part was finding a way to break out of that rut we had gotten ourselves into. We needed a plan.

You never know who you'll impress by doing what job, so my philosophy has always been to do the best work I could, keeping my integrity at all times. I also came in on time, with a smile. Whenever I put my name on something, I make sure it is top quality. "Your work is your signature" has always been my stance in business.

I already held every license under the sun, which was unusual in our line of work. I was NICET Level IV certified for fire-alarm systems, one of just a few in our state at that time. In addition, I was licensed for fire alarms, burglar alarms, access control, as well as various other miscellaneous and helpful licenses in Oklahoma.

The big companies usually wanted us to go out with their logo on our truck and work shirts, but, from the beginning, I refused. I knew we had to brand ourselves if we were ever going to break out of the subcontracting work. I needed people to know that Stampsco was responsible for their installation.

A while back, we'd been hired to subcontract work for another alarm company whose client had an enormous barbecue restaurant. It was an extremely complicated property, requiring a lot of work. Not only did they have an old log cabin that needed rewiring, there were several other buildings spread out across their fifteen-acre property.

One day, I got a call, a referral from an industry professional, who had been a part of that restaurant job. He asked me if we might take a look at another challenging job, a four-story apartment complex for the elderly.

One of our competitors had gone in and fried the system. It was in bad shape, with battery acid spewed everywhere. They were fined heavily by the State inspector and the local fire marshal, but that didn't help the client any. They needed a working system quickly.

Since it was an obsolete system, we couldn't just order parts for it. Once we did a thorough inspection, we couldn't see any way around replacing everything. The system needed a complete upgrade.

The owners were on a thirty-day fire watch, which meant they had to pay to have a fireman out on the site at all times, twenty-four-seven. At twenty-five dollars an hour, it added up, so they were motivated to get the system installed and under code as soon as humanly possible.

Most projects we get aren't quite as urgent as this one was. One usually has more time, but since the safety of the elderly residents was on the line, we all felt the pressure to bring it up to code quickly. Not only were we getting paid well, but we were saving lives.

Since the fire marshals had given the owners thirty days to handle the fire-protection system, that timeline was set in stone. It was a bit of an impossible task, but, fortunately, we were just wrapping up the two other projects on our schedule, so we could afford to devote all our time to this project.

We hired a new man, Bobby, who was a find. Tony had worked with him on another job and managed to recruit him over to Stampsco in the nick of time. With Tony, Sean, and Bobby, I knew we could get it all done.

Normally, we'd need at least two weeks just to draw up the designs for a project of this magnitude, but with the time constraint we had, we couldn't take longer than a week. Paige and I hand-drew the designs first; then I created a Computer-Aided Design (CAD) version to submit to the fire marshal for approval. Fortunately, I had taught myself CAD during the evenings.

Two days after I submitted the designs for approval with the fire marshal's office, they sent it back, marveling at how nice a design it was. "It's so much better than the crayon drawings we're used to getting from other companies."

I grinned. It was nice to get a pat on the back once in a while.

I arranged for a few family friends to pick up the girls from school for the next few weeks and then sat down with my team, letting them know there would be a lot of overtime. The girls were happy because they got to go to the zoo, swim, and generally have fun.

Everyone was jazzed about that, except for Sean, who seemed to be perpetually bent out of shape. I didn't have time to delve into what was wrong with him, but I knew I needed to keep an eye on him. As the project progressed, I had to speedily wrap up a couple other subcontracted ones. All throughout the work, I never missed a beat with my protocol.

Many days, we all worked side by side. I always stayed on site as long as I could but typically had to cut out early. One day, when I was packing up to go, after about seven hours of hard labor, Sean looked like a thundercloud had just opened up above him.

"What do you mean, you're leaving?" he asked.

"I have to go," I replied. I didn't want to tell him that I had to get my coffee enema in before four o'clock. It's what my daughters and her friends would have deemed "TMI" (Too Much Information).

"I have other obligations, but I'll be back."

"We're under the gun! We can barely get this done if we all work fifteen hours a day. If you and Paige take off, we don't have a prayer."

Who do you think you're talking to, buddy?

I quickly bit back my anger. He was working his tail off, and we needed him. Part of my job was motivating everyone. "Don't worry. We'll get it all done."

He turned his back on me and sulked back to work, but I could hear him faintly mutter, "You're throwing us to the wolves." I thought about chasing him down but realized it was best to just leave.

He was right, though. There was a ton of pressure coming from the owners, who were under the gun to complete the project within thirty days. Everyone feared a fire. From the beginning, I warned them that we'd do our best but that I couldn't promise the proposed timeline. I knew I'd be close, though.

One of the challenges of the building was all the beautiful crown molding along the ceilings. We had to hand cut it, in order to get the cabling through the wall into each of the 101 apartments. It wasn't speedy work.

One of the nice perks was that the patrons loved us. It was such rewarding work. I think it was probably the most excitement they had seen in years. Some of them would follow us around the facility, while others would invite us to eat lunch with them in their cafeteria. They all seemed full of questions for us.

Tony, being young and fit, caught the attention of a few ladies. One in particular would get all dolled up each day to see him. She would paint her lips with bright-red lipstick, which would end up being a bit smeared around the edges. Then she'd follow him around all day.

A few of the bolder ladies would pinch him on the butt while he was on a ladder. Tony took it all in stride and was polite to everyone, showing off his southern charm.

Everything went smoothly, except for one day when Paige went out to the truck by herself to get a few tools. When she came back, her face was beet red, and she was muttering under her breath.

"What happened?" I asked, stepping down the ladder as quickly as I could.

"Men!"

"What happened?" I repeated, gently.

"One of the electricians wouldn't let me pass. I was digging around in the back of the truck, and he approached me. I told him to move, but he gave me this look, and I didn't like it."

I held my breath. "Did he lay a finger on you?" I was ready to have a few words with the man if he had.

"No," she said. "He just cornered me and asked a bunch of insulting questions about why I was there and if I really thought I was qualified."

"Did you tell him how the cow eats the cabbage?"

She nodded her head. "He seemed floored to learn that I'm a licensed fire-alarm tech. He stopped bothering me after that."

I relaxed and pulled Paige into my arms. "Some of these guys are knuckleheads. Just ignore them."

"I know."

"Look—let's just agree to always stick together."

"That's not possible," she said.

"Well, we can be within earshot."

"Yeah, I guess."

"Certainly no more trips to the truck without me—okay?" I said, pulling back so I could look her in the eye.

Paige nodded, and we both got back to work. The next day, Paige came in dressed in baggy clothes, with a bandana wrapped around her head, but it didn't stop the other workers from making a racket when they saw her. When we came in after lunch, most of the crew were still on break. We had to walk through them to get to our station. They were catcalling like crazy, despite her carefully rumpled look.

I turned to her to gauge her reaction. Although she looked to be taking it in stride, I said, "I can never get these guys to stop whistling at me. I'm really glad you're here to protect me!"

She gave me a big smile and stayed close by as we worked through the afternoon.

I did my best to check on the other guys now and then. It was becoming clear that Sean was having trouble. He often looked like death warmed over, and he was showing up late a lot.

"Sean, what's going on with you?" I asked one day.

"A lot of stuff," he grumbled. "I got a DUI a while back, and it's been rough."

"Be straight with me. Are you drinking on the job?"

"No," he said. "I wouldn't do that."

"Okay, because I need you at your best here. We're counting on you."

"Right," he said, not looking me in the eye.

"Not exactly the enthusiastic answer I was looking for," I said.

He glared at me. "It doesn't help that I have to work fifteen hours a day, and you come in and out when you feel like it."

I hadn't told Sean that I had cancer. So many people looked at me differently when I told them. They seemed to judge me, treating me like some kind of victim. I did my best to contain the rumors, but I realized it was time to let him know.

"Have a seat," I said.

Sensing the shift in my mood, he quieted down and took a seat on a folding chair. "What is it?"

"I have cancer."

Okay, maybe that was a bit blunt.

"I was diagnosed last September, and I've been fighting it ever since."

His mouth dropped open. "Whoa!"

"Puts things in perspective, doesn't it?"

"Yeah, man. I'm sorry. I didn't know!"

"I know," I said. "And I would appreciate it if you didn't share that with anyone."

"You got it, boss. I just can't believe it."

"That's why I need to leave early each day. I've got to do my protocol. It's not that I'm being lazy, it's that I need to stay on my scheduled treatments to survive."

He turned red and put his head in his hands. "I'm so sorry. I've been such a jerk."

"Don't worry about it. But I could really use your help."

He nodded his head vigorously and then looked up at me. "Yeah, of course! Hey, I'll work extra hours if you need me to."

True to his word, Sean stepped it up a notch. He arrived on time and worked with renewed energy for about a week. Unfortunately, he slid downhill again after that.

I was on another site when Bobby called to tell me that he thought Sean was drunk.

Not what I need to hear.

I dropped what I was doing and went over to the job site. Sean saw me and groaned.

As I got close to him, I could smell alcohol on his breath. "Are you drunk?"

"I didn't drink this morning," he said. His bloodshot eyes told a different story. He swayed as he looked at me.

"How on earth did you get here?"

"In my truck."

I threw my hands up in the air. "But they put a breathalyzer in there after your DUI, so that you're not able to drive drunk. How the heck did you get around that failsafe?"

"When I couldn't get the car to start, I had a neighbor breathe into it for me. I knew you needed me, man, so I figured it was the right thing to do."

"Are you telling me that you had so much to drink last night that you were too drunk to drive this morning?"

He looked down at the ground. "I guess."

"I can't have you on the site like this, you know."

He looked like he might cry. "Don't fire me."

"I have no choice," I said. "And I can't have you drive home like this."

"I'm okay."

"What? No, you're not! Look—if you get in that car, I'll call the police, and you'll be arrested."

He looked like I'd just slapped him hard across the face. "Okay, okay. I'll have my friend pick me up."

I asked Bobby to keep an eye on him. I didn't trust him not to climb into his car and try to drive home the second I was out of sight. Once I was confident the situation was handled, I went back to the other job site. It would be tough with one man down, but we'd have to manage without him.

PAIGE

WHEN WE COMPLETED THE LAST TWO SUBCONTRACTING JOBS for Mariner, Rodney and I agreed that we were finally in a position where we could end things with that company. The combination of being forced to install improperly designed systems and working with their antagonistic managers was just too much. We'd still take a few subcontracting jobs here and there with other companies, just not with Mariner.

I submitted all the invoices to Mariner and waited for the check. When it didn't arrive, Rodney called their headquarters. The woman in billing gave him some song and dance about how they were switching to a new company-wide system, so the computers weren't working properly. They weren't sure when they would be able to cut our check. She actually told us to wait and be patient. We rolled our eyes and drove out to their headquarters to try to collect our money personally.

It wasn't hard to find the woman we'd talked to on the phone. She was in her mid-fifties and wore small, wire-framed glasses.

"It's like I told you on the phone," she said. "We can't cut you a check right now. We'll let you know the moment we can."

"Are you getting your paycheck?" Rodney asked.

She blinked at him and then said, "Of course."

"And I see that the electricity is on and your phones are working, so might I assume that you're able to pay your utility bill?"

Her eyes turned into slits, and her lips pressed into a thin line; she dropped any pretense of being civil.

"Look, you'll get paid when corporate pays you. I can't do anything about it!" It was clear that we weren't getting anywhere with her.

Walking out of the office, I said, "You know we'll have to hire an attorney. We can't let them get away with this."

"Yeah, I think you're right."

"I could sort of understand their refusal to help with your treatment, but then they threatened to fire you, because you have cancer. And if that weren't bad enough, they harassed us every step of the way while we worked for them. And now they're withholding payment!"

What kind of sadistic pleasure could they get from doing all that?

"They have to know very well that we need that money for your treatment. I don't know about you, but I'd be happy if we never worked with them again."

"There's no way I'm taking another project with Mariner," Rodney said. "Besides, it's not like we need them anymore. We have plenty of business with clients who respect us and will treat us fairly."

"Good!" It was like a giant weight had been lifted off my shoulders.

The next day, our lawyer wrote a letter threatening to put a lien on the high-rise property. We were paid within a week.

There. That wasn't so hard, now, was it?

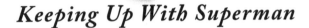

CHAPTER 19

Keeping Up With Superman

PAIGE

WHEN RODNEY WAS DIAGNOSED, WE BOTH REALIZED that I needed to train myself up on all aspects of the business. Although we were doing everything to save Rodney, the very real statistics were looming in our faces. We had to consider that things might not go as planned, and I needed to be able to take over and run Stampsco on a moment's notice. There was a lot to learn, but I have always enjoyed throwing myself into a steep learning curve.

When the Lexington Assisted Living Facility project came to us as a referral from another client, I realized the job would be perfect for me to get my feet wet as a project manager. It was a one-story building with about a hundred rooms, a large project, but pretty straightforward.

"I think it's time for me to run a project," I said. "I've looked over the plans and specifications on this one and really think I can do it."

"You're more than ready," Rodney said.

The biggest challenge was convincing the client that I could handle it. There were just so few women in our industry. I sometimes felt invisible during client meetings. I think people assumed that I was Rodney's secretary, eye candy, or something.

The first step to secure the Lexington client was to go over the details on the project. Although I didn't know the owner personally, I knew her by reputation. She was very well known as a top-notch, no-nonsense businesswoman.

Excited to be managing my first project, I researched her on the Internet before our meeting. She held multiple degrees and ran her company with competence and efficiency. Hopefully, she'd be able to overlook the fact that I had mammary glands and not hold that against me.

My heart raced as Rodney and I walked through the double doors of her large corporate building. The owner happened to be walking out as we were entering. She was flanked by a group of men in pinstriped business suits.

I smiled at her, and she completely ignored me. Instead, she looked Rodney directly in the eye.

"I'll be with you in five minutes. Theresa will show you into the boardroom." She then turned and walked out the same doors I had just come through.

I stood there rooted to a marble square in the lobby, watching her walk away.

Even women find me invisible.

Fine. I'd just make sure she noticed just how qualified I was. It was just another challenge, and I was up for it.

After a few minutes, she came into the boardroom, sat down, and started going over the specifics of the project. She was a natural leader, someone who commanded attention, and she directed every bit of her communication to Rodney. When she finished, Rodney turned to me and allowed me to lead the conversation.

The woman dutifully shifted her attention to me and listened. I went over the entire project with her, breaking down everything that we'd do. After I was done, she turned to Rodney and asked three questions in rapid fire. Rodney, in turn, deflected her questions to me. When I answered her, she then asked more questions, again addressing Rodney.

I need to do something different.

I had to prove that I was an equal owner of Stampsco, fully qualified to run this project. I needed to take back the reins of control on this conversation.

"Do you have ceiling fans in all the rooms?" I asked her.

Her brows furrowed. "What difference does that make?"

"Well, the code states that smoke detectors must be at least three feet away from the blade tips of the ceiling fans, but your drawings don't show them, which is why I asked."

She tilted her head and looked at me. "I didn't know that."

"I'll need a reflected ceiling plan, the plan showing the details of the ceiling."

She paused for a moment. "I'll get it to you this afternoon. Anything else?"

I had her full attention now. Good!

"Will there be a nurses' station?"

"Sure."

"Will it be attended twenty-four seven?"

"Yeah, I guess so."

I detailed out what we'd need to do for that, as there are certain requirements for a station like that. I made sure to explain all the technical jargon.

"Hey, Paige," she said.

Yes, she remembered my name. That's a plus point!

"Let me ask you something. I want to lock down the exit doors in certain sections, so the elderly don't wander off. Can I do that?"

I shook my head. "Fire code will not allow you to lock down egress doors permanently, but there are other solutions. I'd suggest putting alarms on the doors, which would alert the staff when the doors are opened. You could also consider installing electronic locks with a delay on the doors, so that the nurses are warned when someone is trying to leave. We just don't want to lock people in if there's a fire."

"That completely makes sense!"

As we talked back and forth, she asked me more questions, and I answered them. Somewhere along the line, she had stopped addressing Rodney and totally focused on me. Her tone changed subtly, and I knew that she was beginning to respect me as a professional equal.

When we left the office, I went straight home to research the costs for labor and equipment. I worked with Rodney on the bid, because I tended to bid too high. Rodney reminded me that she'd be getting quotes from competitors, which were bound to be much lower.

"Okay, but I refuse to bid so low that we lose money."

"Of course not," he said with a smile.

It took two days to get all the details organized. When we were ready, we scheduled another meeting with her. I knew from experience that it was always a good idea to give the client a bid face to face. That way, you could carefully watch his or her expression. If they keeled over dead, you'd know instantly you'd bid too high.

I handed her the bid and held my breath. She stared at it for a few moments before she looked up at me. "You do realize that you're a good twenty thousand over your competitors, right?"

"There's a reason our clients refer their friends to us. It's because of our expertise and our workmanship. We're very good at what we do, and we don't cut corners."

She looked back at the bid. "It's just a lot more than I'd budgeted."

Rodney leaned forward. "Aren't you glad we spent the time to give you an accurate quote, so you know exactly how much it will really cost you to do it right?"

She laughed. "Okay, you win. If my colleague hadn't raved so strongly about you, I would never consider it. But as it is, he says you're the best in the business."

Although on paper the job seemed straightforward, I quickly realized that the owner wasn't always on the up and up with me. For instance, she failed to mention the indoor swimming pool that she was trying to sneak by the inspectors.

And there were other issues. When we did the walk-through, she pointed out the various rooms. Since the building was still under construction, we could only see its skeleton, so I had to rely heavily on the blueprints to determine the room count.

About halfway through the project, Tony called me. "This building doesn't look anything like the plans."

My adrenaline shot up. "What do you mean?"

"Well, for starters, there's a whole row of rooms on the back end of the building, on the north side."

"Okay, that's not so bad. What's the problem?"

"They aren't on the plans!"

"What?" I cried.

"I swear—they aren't there."

"Are you sure you didn't read the plan wrong?"

"Paige, I know how to read a plan. I'm sure. They aren't there."

"I'll be down there within the hour," I said. Sure enough, it became very clear that she was trying to add eight more rooms that didn't appear on the drawings.

When I confronted her, her lips formed a straight line. "I told you to do a walk-through!"

What are you trying to pull?

"Of course, we did a walk-through," I said, keeping my voice calm. *She's the client.* "You were there when we did. But one often can't see much in the early stages of construction."

In the end, I hit her up for a change order. She wasn't happy, but I don't know what she expected. *Yeah, we'll just add eight rooms to the job for free, because you're trying to pull one over on us. I don't think so.*

A week later, I got a call from the fire marshal, telling us the project had received a stop-work order. They asked us to come to a meeting with various city officials and the client. We were there to answer questions about the fire-protection aspect.

I prepared myself to stay neutral in this war. Rodney and I maintained that we always did exactly what was required by law. I was careful not to take sides.

When my client made it clear that she'd be happy to move the project to another city, the city officials compromised. They sorely needed the tax revenue. It amazed me how quickly the white piece of paper ordering us to stop working was removed from the front door.

We lost one day, which wasn't bad in the larger scheme of things. It could have been worse. The project went pretty smoothly beyond that point.

The day before we were to do the final test with the client, Rodney asked his usual question. "Did you check, double-check, and recheck?"

I grinned. "Yeah."

"What do you think will happen when you flip the switch for the first time?"

"I guess we'll have to wait and see."

"Think a sheet rocker drilled a nail through one of your wires?" he teased.

"Only if they went in there after I left today!"

"If I were a betting man, I'd bet on you," he said, giving me a kiss.

"And you'd win," I replied.

The next day, the test run went perfectly, and the client was very happy. She knew every aspect of our work was precisely to code and would work on into the future. And to top things off, we'd come in ahead of schedule.

One down, the rest of the world to go.

CHAPTER 20

Who Is This Guy, Anyway?

RODNEY

OUT OF NECESSITY, PAIGE HAD TAKEN ON THE ROLE of an enforcement officer, helping me get through those tough times. As the enzymes kicked in, my mood started shifting. Sometimes I felt like I was someone else, some cranky old guy who would get nasty at the drop of a hat. I did my best to control my outbursts, though I'm afraid I imagined my behavior was a bit like PMS on steroids. Pamela explained that it was the enzymes, not me, but that didn't make it any easier for me or my family.

Every day as I choked down mountains of green salad—no dressing, mind you—and steamed vegetables, I would remind myself that I was building health. When my stomach threatened to erupt, I thought about the little Samurai warriors and their need for nutrition to defeat the enemy within. "Stay the course, Rodney," I'd think to myself.

But one day, I'd had enough of the diet. "I don't want this rabbit food," I growled, pushing the plate of organic mixed greens back at Paige with a little too much force.

She didn't back down and was unfazed. She wasn't afraid of me. She wasn't afraid of anyone. She pushed the salad back toward me with a determined look. "You're going to eat this."

I grunted something unintelligible and walked into the living room to sulk.

Who does she think she is, telling me what to eat? Men weren't made to eat a bunch of lettuce on a plate.

She called after me, as calm as could be, "You need to eat this. I'm not fixing anything else, you know. You can choose to either eat it fresh now or all wilted later on. That's up to you."

I stomped back into the dining room and just stuck my face in the plate and started chomping loudly. "*Moo . . .*" I said while glaring at her.

"I get it," Paige said rolling her eyes. "You're a grazing cow, aren't you?"

Looking at the spotless kitchen, I noticed the juicer was still covered with carrot bits from the last juicing.

"Hey, Paige!" I said, feeling a twinge of maliciousness creep over me.

"What is it?" she asked, as she wiped down the counter.

"The least you could do is keep a clean house. Look at that juicer!" I knew this was a low blow for my wife. Ever since the diagnosis, she'd had a cleaning bug that could have been called an obsession. She couldn't rest until the house was in mint condition.

She glanced at the juicer. "I guess it's time for your juice." Her voice was a little too sweet, too calm. She started to prepare the carrots, kale, and other veggies for my drink.

"You'd think you could remember to clean out the juicer!"

I continued to force the salad down my throat, gagging on it a few times, loudly. The juicer was making such a racket, I could hardly be heard. I decided to wait until it was done before I said anything else. There was really no point in complaining to myself.

When she was done, I resumed my diatribe. "I mean, the least you could do is clean the juicer! It's a mess, filthy. How hard is that, anyway?"

"Sweetie?" she said, as she poured the liquid into the blender. "Yeah?"

She went to the freezer and pulled out a bag of those blasted liver chunks. I was never going to get used to that flavor in my drink.

Disgusting, vile things.

She gave me a crocodile smile, as she shook the bag. I watched her walk over to the blender and drop one cube in. I made a face, but I knew I could handle one chunk. Any more than one was complete torture to get down.

Watching me, she glanced at the juicer pointedly and dropped another chunk in.

There it was. My punishment.

I glared at her, standing up. "You vindictive little . . ."

Her lips were curled into a smug little smile as she dropped a third chunk of liver into the potion.

I fell back into my chair, speechless.

Three? I can't handle three.

My stomach churned violently at the thought.

"Want more?" she asked.

"No!" I cried in horror, shaking my head as hard as I could.

"Did you want to say anything else to me, Rodney dearest?"

I sighed, "I'm sorry." I was, too. I realized that I deserved three liver chunks for my behavior.

She nodded with approval. "Is our house a mess?"

"No," I said. "You know it isn't. It's the cleanest house on the block. It's the enzymes talking."

"I know," she said, coming over to give me a hug. "But you must remember to be nice to the person making your juice."

"I've learned my lesson," I said with a laugh. I gave her a kiss to cement my apology.

"Good!"

I pulled back and shook my head, staring into the drink. "Paige, three liver chunks?"

"Yes, my dear," she said. "Maybe next time you'll control your temper a little better!"

I managed to swallow the whole thing, which I think surprised Paige a little. I couldn't waste it—not after she'd gone through so much trouble for me. Besides, we couldn't exactly afford to throw anything away.

I guess I have to take my medicine . . .

PAIGE

I TOOK NO PLEASURE IN MY ROLE AS A FOOD NAZI. But with the grim reaper stalking us relentlessly, I had no choice. It plagued me to see him tormented, not just with pain but with intense cravings for meat and other "normal"—translate "toxic"—foods. The prospect of the unremitting grief the girls and I might have to endure without him drove me to take charge when I had to. Too much was riding on his beating this thing. The crushing fear of being left without him, the fear for the girls losing their father, the fear of having to run the company alone never let me rest.

Honestly, I don't know how he did it. He was really beyond good. For a solid year, he was on the most stringent diet and most stringent schedule imaginable, while working 80-hour weeks most of the time. And he didn't deviate, not a hair. Finally, after the one-year mark, he was allowed to introduce more foods into his diet. He could have some meat occasionally, and we could eat out once in a while, but Pamela had warned me to make sure he went easy on his diet changes. We all breathed a huge sigh of relief. With that in mind, if he ever ordered the wrong thing, I'd have to set him straight. I became a bit of a tyrant, I'm afraid, making sure that he didn't eat too many bad things at once.

One time, when we went to our favorite Mexican restaurant down the street, he tried to order a steak burrito with extra sour cream.

I turned to the waitress and said, "Make that a grilled chicken salad—hold the sour cream."

He turned to me, his eyes mere slits. "What?"

Get angry all you like—you're not ordering cancer on a plate.

"You heard me."

"I'll order whatever I want," he huffed. "I've earned that."

"You can order anything you like, as long as it somewhat follows the protocol."

The poor waitress looked like she'd rather be anywhere else than taking our order. I felt for her, but there was no way I was backing down. I also wasn't about to explain my rationale to her.

"So, what will it be?" The poor lady's voice trembled a little.

I repeated my version of his order and glared at him, daring him to speak out again. I knew him well enough to know that he wouldn't continue to battle me in public, and he knew me well enough to know that I would. In the end, I won, and she brought the food I requested.

There were times when he'd try to wrangle a steak from me and I would relent once a year, on his cancer anniversary. We'd get a small, expensive organic steak for him, and he'd gulp it down in one bite.

CHAPTER 21

Cancer Down, What Next?

RODNEY

A DAY DIDN'T GO BY WHEN I DIDN'T CONSIDER my three goals. I was in my sixth month on the protocol and felt the first goal was well on its way to becoming a reality. I still had a lot of work ahead of me, but I had personal certainty that I had conquered my illness.

Why not go after one of the other two?

Since I wasn't up for a family vacation yet and was tired of renting our house, I realized that it was time to talk Paige into taking a step toward tackling the third goal.

I have often joked with people that I grew up in the hood, but it isn't too far from the truth. Paige grew up on the other side of the tracks. When we got married, we were struggling, both working two to three jobs just to pay the bills. We counted our pennies, collected coupons, and went without luxuries, so she was wary of extravagances that we couldn't afford and stuck tightly to the budget.

Although Paige was as eager as I to own our own home, I knew that she didn't consider me out of the woods quite yet with my cancer. Still, I figured that it was my body that played host to those little alien creatures, so I was the ultimate expert.

Those mutant cells were toast.

Besides, each time I'd visit Dr. A., he'd confirm that my LDH count, a protein that indicates cancer when elevated, was decreasing drastically. For me, the best visible sign that I was getting better was watching the tumors shrink each month. I could see them expanding with the enzymes and then contracting on the off cycle. With each cycle, they were getting smaller and smaller.

So, it was time to take the necessary steps to achieve our third goal. I didn't want to put it off another day, so one perfect May Saturday, I turned to Paige and said, "It's time to look for a house!"

She gave me a tentative nod. "Sure."

"All I'm suggesting is that we take a nice drive to just start looking around. That's all. I know it will take us time to collect the down payment, so don't worry. It's not like we can buy the property today."

"You know I do love a good, long car ride," Paige said.

We stopped at a convenience store and picked up some realtor guides and maps. Also, a realtor friend of mine had sent me a list of homes earlier in the day. Unfortunately, we made the rookie mistake of hitting a high-end neighborhood first. After looking at several million-dollar homes, all the reasonably priced homes paled in comparison. It just messed with our perception of what we might get for less than our budget.

I became methodical in my planning, plotting on the map the areas we might want to live, highlighting areas we liked and darkening out the neighborhoods that were less desirable.

We finally found one house I liked. Paige didn't care for it but agreed she could live with it. She'd always had a great eye for detail, and this particular home was rather plain.

"It's a box with white walls and no charm. Can't we go up just a little and find something we can like?" A few times, she asked if we could go up in our price range to find something more to her liking, but I stood firm. Since the house met all our basic requirements, I was good to go. It so happened that it was a little over my budget, and we couldn't talk the owners down in price, so we kept looking.

By July, we'd stumbled upon a house that was perfect. Paige and I both loved it, and it was in a perfect neighborhood. After walking through the open house, we talked to the owner, who happened to also be the builder.

"My husband and I built this place with the idea of moving here," she said, "but that plan didn't work out. We couldn't sell the other property, so we're giving this one up."

"We love it," I said. "I'd like to put in an offer."

"Sorry." She gave a little shake of her head. "We just got word that we have a pending contract. It wasn't finalized until an hour ago. I kept the open house, figuring it was better to cover all my bases."

Despite our disappointment, we continued to look for another house, week after week. Another popped up in the same neighborhood that we loved even more, complete with a wrought-iron staircase that stole Paige's heart, but it was way too priccy.

After giving up on that one, we drove past the previous house and discovered the "For Sale" sign was back up. Walking in, we found the same lady, showing the house. "The contract fell through, so it's back on the market," she said. "Still interested?"

"Yeah," I said.

"Can we cut out the realtors, though, and just negotiate together?" she said.

"Sure," I said reluctantly.

In the end, we paid $10,000 more than we wanted to spend. They reduced their asking price by $25,000, bringing it down below the appraised value.

It was perfect, just under 3,000 square feet, with a huge backyard. The only drawback was that there was no pool. I tried to talk her into putting one in, but she shook her head. "I'll throw in a refrigerator, though."

Yeah, that's the same thing.

In the end, we couldn't have been more happy with our purchase. It was a beautiful home. We moved in at just about the one-year anniversary of that fateful doctor's appointment, when Dr. A. told me I had cancer and would have only a few months to live, if I was lucky.

PAIGE

RODNEY AND I REALIZED we had one more item from our original goals list that we needed to do. We'd fought back against cancer and were winning, so now it was time to celebrate.

"Let's go to Disney World in Orlando!" Rodney said one evening, as we were cuddled on the couch.

"Really?" My heart raced as I looked into his eyes. "Are you sure you're up for it?"

He paused and thought about it. "Yeah."

I laughed. "You don't sound very convinced. You know, it'll be strenuous."

"I'll manage," he said. "It can't be harder than climbing up and down ladders all day. It will be fun. Besides, you and the girls deserve a treat."

"It's expensive."

"I know," Rodney said. "However, I've priced it out, and I know we can make it work. There are ways to save money. For instance, if we rent a house, it'll be much cheaper than staying in hotels."

"And so much more convenient! I can cook and juice more easily."

"We'll fly, definitely. It's part of the adventure. Besides, we can use the air miles we've earned on our credit cards, and we don't have to waste precious time driving all that way."

"And the girls have never flown. I bet they'll love it!"

Well, I was half right. Jade loved the idea of flying, but Jessika let us know that she was nervous. As the day of our flight approached, the more obsessed she became, asking us if we were sure planes were safe.

If we had known that she was going to be so afraid, we might have opted to drive, but, as it was, I'd purchased the tickets in advance and couldn't get a refund, so we were locked in.

When we arrived at the airport, I became nervous but for a different reason. We had to pack everything for the protocol in our carry-on bags, and I wasn't sure what the security officers would say when they saw the hundreds of pills and all the odd powders. We had wheat-grass powder, granulated coffee, etc. I hoped they wouldn't stamp it all "Unknown Substances" and detain us or confiscate it. I was very relieved when they let it pass without a single question.

Jessika and I sat together on the plane, but I'm afraid I wasn't too sympathetic to her plight. Jade, on the other hand, was having a blast, raising her hands like she was on a roller coaster and calling out for more turbulence. Jessika groaned when she heard that.

We arrived on a Saturday and decided to stay in that Sunday and enjoy the place. We had a cookout and hung by the pool. Since we didn't have a pool at home, the kids were ecstatic.

The following day, we went to the Magic Kingdom. It was my first time there, so we made sure to arrive the moment the gates opened. Rodney had been there only once as a kid, when his father had taken him. His grandfather accompanied them also, and it was a treasured memory, because, soon after that, he passed away from prostate cancer. But the good sport that he was, his grand-dad went on rides with him all day, creating lifelong memories that Rodney has cherished ever since. We both wanted similar beautiful memories for our girls.

As we took the large ferry boat over from the parking lot, the girls' eyes went wide with excitement. I caught Rodney watching them, soaking in their enthusiasm.

They might have been happy just riding the ferry back and forth all day. They pointed at every little thing, interested in all aspects of the journey. It was fun to watch.

When we arrived at the park, there was a good-sized line. I guess others had the idea to arrive early, too. I was glad that we had purchased the tickets ahead of time.

We started by taking the train around the property, getting a better feel for what was there. The girls were most intrigued by the princesses, so we spent quite a bit of time with the different characters, getting their autographs and taking pictures with them.

Fantasyland was incredible. The girls were entranced by all the fairytales coming to life throughout the park. Jade wanted to figure out how everything was put together, how it ran, and how the special effects worked. Jessika just marveled at it all.

Unfortunately, the lines were rather long, and, as the day wore on, I could see that Rodney was getting a little pale. While we waited in line for the "It's a Small World" ride, he found a place to sit and wait. I didn't even bother to suggest that he let the staff know how sick he'd been. I'm sure they would have let him go to the front of the line, but Rodney would rather suffer through it than tell anyone.

Back when he had first been diagnosed, he was given a cancer discount card to use at restaurants and participating stores. It was typically for chemo patients, but his doctor gave him one anyway.

"Look, I can buy all kinds of cancer-causing things with this," he said as he threw it in the garbage.

Food was a huge problem for him. While away from the rental house, we had to rely on restaurant food. After having eaten so carefully for the last year and a half, it was nerve wracking to eat non-organic food. Our solution was to sneak in nuts and other organic snacks and try not to eat much else throughout the day.

As the day progressed, I could tell Rodney was exhausted and nauseated, and I suggested we leave early, but he flatly refused. He didn't want the girls to miss the Main Street Electric Light Parade. It was one of the top experiences that he remembered fondly from his previous trip.

In the end, he survived, and the girls never knew how much he was struggling. It was completely worth the hassle. Jessika and Jade couldn't stop talking about the amazing parade of lights all week.

The rest of the week was a dream. We went to Hollywood Studios, Animal Kingdom, and Sea World. I couldn't believe how many amazing parks there were in that city. We could have spent another week in Orlando and not have seen everything.

Rodney had a lot of fun seating us in the Splash Zone at Sea World. When Shamu came by, we got drenched, and Rodney thought that was the funniest thing.

I wasn't big on roller coasters, but somehow Jessika convinced me to go on one at that park called "The Kraken." It was one of those rides where your feet dangle under you. I shook my head for a good ten minutes before I finally relented. It's so hard to deny my little girl anything.

Jade joined us, sitting directly in front of me. Just as we sat down, Jessika panicked. She didn't like her legs dangling. I made eye contact with the attendant and then asked him to let her off. He took pity on her and unlocked her seat. I, on the other hand, was in for the ride of my life. I think I screamed the entire time.

And how is this fair?

The week went by in a flash, and, suddenly, I found myself back at the airport, standing in line at the security station. For some reason, the officer took a stronger interest in all the vials we had with us this time. He opened the wheat grass powder and managed to spill it all over my clothes. I was never able to get those stains out.

On the plus side, Jessika seemed less freaked out by the flight back. Maybe all those roller coasters had tamed her stomach.

It was a good thing that Rodney had two days to recoup at home before he had to tackle work at the office again. We were all pretty exhausted. It's one of those ironic things in life: You always seem to need to rest up after a vacation.

CHAPTER 22

Reaching Out

RODNEY

A MONTH AFTER THE ORLANDO TRIP, I was due for my quarterly checkup with Dr. A. I wasn't looking forward to it, because the smell of the chemo treatments really got to me, and I worried about using the restroom, because of the radiation exposure with the patients. My research showed that patients who receive radiation therapy can poison others around them shortly after the treatment. I couldn't afford to take any chances.

However, keeping the appointments was important. Now that I was on the other side of things, I really wanted to see the original CT scan from September 2005, when I was first diagnosed. Dr. A. was reluctant but finally gave in.

The scan showed I'd apparently had a tumor in my abdomen that was three inches by three inches. A normal lymph node should be about the size of a pea or bean. That really freaked me out. There were dozens of other, smaller tumors that I had no idea were there, including fifteen in my neck and twenty in my chest.

Peering into the images, I noticed a black spot on my liver. "What's that?"

"It was just a small cyst," he said. "Probably nothing to worry about."

"I never knew it was there!"

"Well, there's no need to worry about any of it, because they're all gone now," he said, shaking his head. "You're a walking miracle!"

We continued to see Dr. A. on a quarterly basis until we hit the two-year mark. At that time, he let me know that we could come in on an annual basis. He wanted to check in with me at least once a year to make sure everything continued to progress smoothly.

At the two-year visit, I noticed that the red-headed nurse looked tired and withdrawn, when she was normally vibrant, doing everything she could to cheer those around her up.

Hesitant to overstep any boundaries, but knowing something was wrong, I said, "Is everything okay?"

"Sure," she said, not meeting my eye.

"Uh, okay," I said. "It's just that you look a bit down. Is there anything I can do?"

She sighed and looked up at me. "I have breast cancer."

I gasped. "Oh, I'm so sorry!"

"That's horrible," Paige echoed. "I can't believe it."

"Thank you," she said with a slight smile. "I appreciate your thoughtfulness."

"What are you doing for it?" I asked. It would be a dream to be able to help her through Dr. Kelley's protocol, but I knew she probably would reject my advice. Still, I wanted to open the door and let her know that I was willing to help her.

"I started my first round of chemotherapy this week," she said.

"I'm sure it will all work out," I said.

"Thank you," she said. "Dr. A. will be in shortly."

She paused for a moment, glancing up and down my body before she left the room. Suffering through chemotherapy, I'd imagine that she probably felt a little jealous that I hadn't had to go through what she'd have to go through.

When the door closed behind the nurse, Paige whispered, "You did the right thing. Talking to her about the protocol now would probably just upset her."

"You're right," I said, staring at the door she'd just left through. "I wish we could help her."

"Yeah, I know."

When I went home that evening, I logged onto a few of the cancer forums I'd been tracking. So many people wrote in daily with their cancer story, detailing their illnesses. Since I had managed to escape death, I felt a responsibility to share my story with others, possibly offering hope. I began chatting back and forth with various people about options.

Then, out of the blue a few weeks later, my cousin wrote me, asking if I might help a friend of hers. Her friend had a forty-year-old son, Jason, who had just been diagnosed with Non-Hodgkin's Lymphoma. I emailed her back immediately, encouraging her to have Jason contact me, eager to help someone else going through what I had just experienced.

Hopefully, my story might save a life or two.

Jason's father wrote me first, letting me know that his son was eager for a natural cure. I noticed that he'd put "natural cure" in quotes, which told me he was a traditional-medicine advocate. I assumed the whole subject was an explosive topic for the family.

The first thing I did was to arm the family with information, giving them half a dozen websites to research. I briefly told them my story, letting them know that I'd been pressured to do chemo but had chosen against that treatment option.

I created a starter list of things that I could recommend to anyone with cancer. They included things like: Stop eating animal meat for a few months, quit all forms of sugar, cut out white flour and white rice, start on Dr. Kelley's recommended diet, begin juicing immediately, detoxify through coffee enemas, build and use a near-infrared sauna, exercise regularly, and get plenty of good sleep.

Reading over my email a few times, I worried that I might scare them off. I tried to edit it down but realized I couldn't. It was all important, so I sent it anyway. Within a few days, Jason responded, asking if we could talk on the phone. He sounded relieved to know that I had come out of this debilitating disease alive.

"It's good to hear your voice," he said. He sounded a lot more upbeat than I'd expected.

"I'm glad you're in good spirits!" I said.

"You're an inspiration!"

That made my day. "Thank you, Jason! I can tell you that it took a lot of hard work and dedication, but I'm happy to say that I came out on the other side. You can, too."

"The oncologists are telling me I'm a prime candidate for chemo, being that I'm young and strong."

Of course, they did.

"Chemo seems to be their only option."

"Yeah, I know," Jason said. "That's one of the reasons I really wanted to talk to you. I wanted options."

"It's great that you're taking responsibility for your own treatment. So many people turn their lives over to the men in the white coats."

"Yeah—not me. I tried to talk to one oncologist about natural treatments. Do you know that he walked out of the room?"

I whistled low. "No way! That's incredible. Did he ever come back?"

"Nope," he said. "My wife and I waited a good thirty minutes before we figured that he'd just bailed on us. We left the hospital and didn't go back."

"I was fortunate and really happy to find my doctor. Dr. A.'s not a fan of 'charlatan medicine,' as he calls it, but he allowed me to make my own decisions and still continues to see me."

"Wow, that doctor's a keeper! I might be more willing to see an oncologist if I could find one like that."

"We're blessed to have Dr. A.," I said. "And he does readily admit that I'm rid of the cancer."

The conversation went on for another hour. I felt that I'd had a positive impact, but I didn't hear back from him for a full month, as he went on a long vacation and saw a few more specialists. He continued to sound cheerful in his emails, but I worried. He was carrying a ticking time bomb in his blood that needed to be addressed.

I encouraged him to talk to Pamela as soon as possible, so that he could learn more about the protocol. The worst thing you can do with cancer is sit by and wait, so I hoped he would pursue some course of action immediately. He half-heartedly tried to reach Pamela over the next month but said they kept missing each other.

When I found out that Jason was coming to my area on business, I invited him out for dinner one evening. It was nice to put a face to the voice and emails.

After that evening, I didn't hear back from him for a full four months. When I finally did get an email from him, he said that he had just signed on with Pamela, having finally purchased Dr. Kelley's book. He apologized for not getting back to me sooner but said he had been on a month-long holiday. While vacations can be therapeutic, I wondered how much further his cancer had progressed.

After chatting with him a bit, I could tell that he had the gist of the protocol. He asked me a few questions about how to build a near-infrared sauna, so I sent him the data again. I breathed a sigh of relief, knowing that he was finally connected with Pamela and armed with the correct information.

Since I had been desperate for referrals from people who had successfully completed Dr. Kelley's program when I first approached Pamela, I offered to be an open testimonial for her. She jumped at the opportunity to hand out my phone number to a select few clients.

"I have one particular client who won't start the program because he can't talk to someone who has gone through it," she said.

"Let me talk to him!" I said.

"I'll ask him. Thank you, Rodney!"

"It's the least I can do. You've done so much for me, and you continue to help so many others. I want to do my part."

Within days, Pamela introduced me to Matthew, a man about my age from California. He'd tried chemo a few times and then stopped, ready for an alternative. Unlike Jason, he didn't dawdle but immediately started up with Pamela, asking me lots of good questions along the way.

He stuck with the program pretty well, and, after a few months, his chest began to swell, just like mine had. Matthew described the tumor as a golf ball sticking out between his ribs. He confided in me that it was a bit alarming to him. I completely understood his fear, having experienced the same exact phenomenon. Pamela and I helped him understand why his tumors might swell like that, and my reassurance made him feel more comfortable. He assured me that he planned to stay the course and continue with the treatment.

When the tumor swelled to the size of a tennis ball, he decided it would be best to consult his oncologist, who was very unsupportive of his choice to decline chemotherapy again. In the meantime, I suggested a few alternative approaches. I continued to encourage him to have a good mental outlook. He needed to know that he could, in fact, beat the cancer.

He continued to monitor his cancer over the summer and got a CT scan, which confirmed that the tumor was localized. Yet, he became more and more nervous about continuing with the enzymes because of the increased swelling. All I could do was offer support and advice based on my experience.

I asked Jason and Matthew if they would like to be introduced to one another, so that they could support each other through the program. It could also help me track Jason's progress while I focused on Matthew.

I was very concerned about Jason, because he'd taken so long to get started with Dr. Kelley's protocol. He seemed bent on taking as many vacations as possible, "enjoying his last days," rather than ensuring he'd live a long life. It was frustrating to watch.

The other thing that troubled me was the dissension among Jason's family members. His brother and father were increasingly concerned about his refusal to consider traditional medicine. Since his father had been the first to reach out to me, he included me in their email conversations. I read email after email, going back and forth between them, watching the tension escalate.

Jason's father couldn't understand why his son didn't monitor his condition with an oncologist. I tried to support Jason by explaining that there were high dosages of radiation that came from each CT scan, which weren't ideal for someone with cancer. But Jason's father was adamant in his belief that doctors wouldn't use something that was dangerous.

Jason didn't handle his parents' concerns very well. It was tough, watching him deal with cancer while fighting with his family. All I could do was remain a stabilizing influence for him and hope his family would calm down.

The good news was that Jason said he was following the protocol exactly. Yet, he had waited more than six months to get started.

If only he had started when we first spoke.

Over the next few months, his tumors expanded. He lost his job and became an angry, bitter man. My guess is that the enzymes weren't helping his mood. I received several emails from his father, who'd become more and more desperate to help Jason.

I encouraged him to support Jason in his chosen treatment plan, reminding him that the medical doctors felt his cancer was incurable, so there was little they could do for his son.

Despite my efforts, Jason and his family continued to battle. Although I could understand the family's concerns, the added pressure of having to constantly explain himself to them was taking its toll. All I could do was continue to listen and be there for him.

Meanwhile, by the end of the summer, Matthew emailed me pictures showing his tumor had expanded to the size of a softball. He was also having dramatic symptoms to go with the huge lump.

Hold the course, my friend!

When Matthew asked me about my opinion of Vitamin C in high doses, I cautioned him that it could be risky. Even though I knew a woman who'd had success with it in the treatment of her bone cancer, I wasn't confident the treatment would work for him. Frightened by the size of the tumor, he decided it was worth the risk and took a chance. Unfortunately, the gamble didn't pay off, and the tumor expanded and spread.

Scared and unsure, he went to his oncologist, who did various tests. In the end, Matthew decided to stop the enzyme protocol and try another round of chemo and radiation.

◆ ◆ ◆

By early October, my cousin wrote to tell me that Jason had been rushed to the hospital. His kidneys had shut down, and he was withering away. The doctors had done their best to give him chemo, but Jason refused. He went off the enzyme protocol and stopped communicating with anyone. A month after that, I learned that he had died. Paige and I sent flowers to his family and mourned his passing.

I continued to keep in touch with Matthew, whose doctor had prescribed chemotherapy and a stem-cell transplant. Matthew stuck with the chemotherapy for a few months, which reduced the tumors. Soon after, he flew to Texas for a stem-cell transplant.

By December, everything seemed to be improving. The family rejoiced and reported that Matthew's appetite had improved. A week later, they sent out emails to their friends, stating that the stem-cell transplant had been a success and that he had been discharged from the hospital.

Paige and I were so relieved. It looked like Matthew had been one of the few to survive that procedure. Yet three months later, his heart stopped beating, a common result of chemotherapy treatment.

Losing Matthew and Jason within months of each other was heartbreaking. Paige and I had become very close with both of them and couldn't believe they were both gone. Cancer is a terrible disease. There are far too few success stories out there.

Despite these setbacks, I continued to consult with people, friends of friends, and referrals from Pamela. To date none of them have survived, but then again, none of them stuck with the protocol.

CHAPTER 23

Onward and Upward

RODNEY

ONCE I HAD FULLY COMPLETED MY INITIAL THREE GOALS on my list, I set higher targets. I wanted Stampsco to continue to expand and reach new heights. That just wasn't possible working from home, so we leased a building and hired a few more employees.

It blew me away to think about how quickly Stampsco had grown. It took many dedicated hours of rolling up our sleeves and diving into hard work, but in the end, we were recognized repeatedly for standing out in our industry.

Although I rarely had time, I realized that I should relax a bit more—maybe even pick up a hobby or two. One day, I happened to notice a man flying a remote-controlled airplane in a large field. I remembered my dad flying model airplanes when I was a kid, so it piqued my interest. I stopped and asked him about it. He was kind enough to give me a private demonstration, and I was immediately hooked.

As luck would have it, the son of the shop owner where I bought my first RC plane happened to be a world-class model airplane pilot. He kindly agreed to help train us. Paige and I found a perfect field nearby, and I had a new outlet for all my day's frustrations.

Looking out over the field one day, a building across the way caught my eye.

"Wow! Wouldn't that be a great place for our office?"

"We just leased a new building a few months ago!" Paige said with a laugh.

"Yeah, I know, but I predict that we'll outgrow that place within a year."

She nodded. "But are we ready to buy a property? That's a big commitment."

"Let's just see what the asking price is," I said, packing up the plane.

We soon discovered that the asking price was way too high to even consider buying, especially since it was a warehouse, which meant it would need some additional construction to make the space usable, and that would require more money. Despite that setback, I kept my eye on the place.

As time wore on, I continued to fly my plane next to the property, visualizing taking over that warehouse for Stampsco. No one was moving in, so I figured I still had a chance.

After a year passed, my prediction for my company came true. We were bursting at the seams at the leased office. Since the warehouse was still up for sale, I worked on the owners, talking them down in price. Then I set up a small-business loan with my bank. It took another eight months to close on the building, but then it was ours.

"We have our new Stampsco headquarters!" I said to Paige. "It's just like I envisioned."

Her eyes twinkled. "You made that happen!"

"*We* made that happen!"

We continued to hire more salespeople. Some went door to door, selling small businesses and homeowners on our services. Others went to larger companies. Investing money in a qualified sales force paid off, and we continued to expand.

One of my strategies was to build a large number of recurring accounts, where clients would pay us a small monthly fee to monitor their systems. Since our customer service was strong, they kept coming back and referring new clients to us.

Recurring accounts are great, because they provide residual income, which would continue for years without a lot of extra labor. I started acquiring a few small businesses with recurring clients, so that we could add to our numbers. Of course, our bread-and-butter was still the design and installation of the larger projects.

As we picked up more and more high-profile projects, we were becoming noticed in our industry. Magazines routinely featured articles about our company and high-profile installations.

We began to be able to cherry-pick our clients, going only with the people who weren't looking to save a dime any way they could, but who were interested in high-quality design and installations that lasted. I wasn't interested in cutting corners when it came to safety. When you make mistakes in our industry, people can die.

One day, we got a call about a huge, challenging project. I had known the owner, Tom, for about a decade and had watched him come up the ranks in his business. He started with a small coin shop and was now one of the top online precious-metals retailers in the world. I'd done some small jobs for him through another company in my subcontracting days, and he thought we were the best thing since sliced bread.

Tom asked us to bid on a security project for his new location, the former Federal Reserve Bank in downtown Oklahoma City. Looking over his current system, I noticed he had two dozen security cameras inside and out, along with several armed guards.

"This system's outdated and doesn't work for us," Tom said. "We need a state-of-the-art video, access-control, and intrusion-detection system. I want you to protect our people and our inventory."

"We can do that, Tom," I said, "but it won't be cheap."

"I know. Could you also make it so that we can check in via an Internet connection that's completely secure?"

"Yeah, sure, but we'll have to design it from scratch. We'll have to customize the entire system."

"That's what I want!"

I shook my head. He had to understand the reality of the situation. "We're probably not going to even come close to other bids. They'll be substantially lower."

"That's fine," he said with a grin. "Look, you have the reputation of being the Special Forces unit of this industry. We need someone who can deploy quickly, because we're on a very tight schedule."

I laughed. "Yeah, I've heard that before. It's very flattering."

Tom laughed with me. "And that's why we want your bid."

Way to fan my ego, Tom.

Just preparing the bid took me three days. One of the biggest challenges was the huge three-foot-thick concrete vault, with five-eighths-inch steel lining. The doors weighed a whopping quarter of a million pounds. Then there were two smaller vaults as well. We would need to drill through them all in order to wire the inside. On top of that, we'd have to deal with the other tenants in the building, including the FBI on the second floor.

I really wanted this job, because it would be a real feather in our cap. Plus, I always like a challenge.

When I had the bid together, I scheduled another meeting with Tom and his security director. We sat down at their conference table, exchanging a few niceties, before I slid the pages of the bid across to him. Tom's smile vanished as he pored over it all. "Really?" His voice sounded thin.

"I told you," I nearly growled in frustration.

There goes the last thirty hours of research and planning down the drain.

I looked over at Paige, who calmly inclined her head in Tom's direction. She didn't look upset. Her eyes implored me to keep my cool, so I steeled my expression and waited for him to finish reading.

Finally, Tom pulled out three other bids he'd received and slid them across the table to me. I glanced through them and rolled my eyes. Each one was about a third of the price of our quote.

What were they thinking?

"Why are theirs so much lower than yours?" he asked me.

His question wasn't accusatory, but I couldn't help but feel frustrated. I threw my hands up in the air. "I have no idea. You'll have to ask them! I'm just telling you what I can do for you based on what you will need."

"You need to break it down so that I can understand," he said.

I took a deep breath and realized he was right. I needed to become Rodney the salesman and forget the other companies with their inferior designs and low-end equipment.

I took my time to explain all the details of the project to him, listing out all the unique challenges this particular project had to offer. Although it was obvious to me, it wasn't to him. I explained how the materials involved with the building were tricky and how I honestly doubted some of the companies he'd approached could even come close to completing a job like this.

Glancing through the other bids, I pointed out various examples of major differences, like how the other companies used outdated analog cameras, while we were bidding with IP (Internet Protocol) megapixel cameras, which provide much better clarity and fit his specific request.

I could tell he was paying attention to everything that I was saying.

When I was finally finished, he asked, "Can you get it done in three weeks?"

"Only if we start now, like today!" I said. "Honestly, it's about as tight as you can get, and we'll be downing gallons of coffee to make it all work, but yes, I have it all calculated out and can promise that we'll come in on time."

Paige glared at me, and I realized she didn't like that I had just sworn to drink gallons of coffee.

It's only an expression, Sweetie.

Tom looked over everything we'd submitted another dozen times before he finally relented, agreeing that we needed to get started immediately. We signed the papers that day and set to work on an almost-unimaginable schedule.

I whistled as I walked out of the building. It was one of our largest, highest-profile projects to date, and I couldn't stop grinning. It was only when I was driving back to the office that the magnitude of the stress involved hit me like a tidal wave. I don't think I could have handled it the year prior, but now, with all our new employees in place and my strength almost back to normal, I was ready.

We had to hit the ground running at a sprint in order to get ahead of schedule. From experience, I was well aware that, even with small projects, unanticipated issues can pop up, creating delays. Although I had no idea what we would encounter on this site, I knew whatever it was would be unexpected and inconvenient.

Mistakes were bound to happen, especially when working at breakneck speeds, so I made sure to put a dedicated project manager onsite for each system we were installing. He would be our quality-control supervisor every step of the way.

"Check, double-check, and recheck!" had always been one of my favorite sayings.

The first week went more smoothly than I'd anticipated. We were on schedule, and there were no problems. However, before I could pat myself on the back too hard, Tom asked if we could add another fifty panic buttons.

"You know that isn't an easy thing to add at this phase, right?" I said, downing my third cup of power juice.

Who needs sleep?

He looked confused. "Why? I mean can't you just add them in?"

"No, I'd need to redesign the security system, because each panic button adds zones to the system, and each needs its own wiring and conduit."

He hesitated. "Will this addition delay things? Or can you still make the deadline and put in the new panic buttons?"

"I think we can do it, but it will cost more."

He beamed at me. "Done!"

The last week, we went full speed and even pulled a few all-nighters, staying out on the site one day for a record twenty-six hours. Despite the blizzard that hit mid-project, we met our deadline, and our client was thrilled.

It was a real test of my newfound health. I pushed myself further than I probably should have, but since it was short term and I had plenty of people backing me up, I passed with flying colors.

Tom was so happy with the job we did that he presented us with a special plaque during his Grand Opening ceremony and referred us to a few colleagues. We received a write-up in a trade magazine, who gave us front-page recognition, along with a four-page color spread with plenty of photographs, showing the vaults and our state-of-the-art equipment. It was exactly the publicity we needed.

◆ ◆ ◆

Now that I was healed and Stampsco had reached a new level of success, I could focus on the people who mattered most to me. Although I told Paige every day that I loved and appreciated her, I wanted to find an extravagant way to express my feelings for her. She deserved that—and more.

When I was sick and broke, Paige stuck by me, never wavering, never failing to let me know how much she loved me. She has always been the perfect partner for me, from the very first moment I fell in love with her.

Over the years, I have had only a few chances to surprise Paige with a gift worthy of her. A year before I was diagnosed, I had found a print of Paige's favorite painting, "The Kiss." It was a lovely piece by Austrian artist Gustav Klimt. It was a giant square painting with a golden, shimmering feeling that matched Paige's eyes.

The tricky part had been to find a way to surprise my wife. As Paige would put it, "You can't surprise me. I can figure everything out!"

Not this time!

I'd timed the delivery for a day I knew she was taking the kids swimming at the neighborhood pool. However, as luck would have it, the FedEx guy was leaving just as she drove back to fix sandwiches for the kids.

I was determined to surprise her, though. When she came in the door, I had on my best poker face. "Hey, Babe," I said, giving her a kiss on the cheek. "Having fun?"

"Yeah, a blast! How's work?"

"Good. I closed two new clients this morning."

"Bravo!" she exclaimed. "Hey, did you see the FedEx guy out front?"

"Yeah," I said, holding my breath. "He dropped some packages off for work."

She nodded. "Okay. Well, I'll be out of your hair in a moment."

Whew! That was a close call.

She left quickly, never suspecting a thing. Fortunately, she didn't go out through the garage. Had she seen the huge six-foot-by-six-foot package, she probably would've started guessing at what was in it.

By the time Paige came back home later that day, I'd hung the painting over the fireplace. She walked in the door, glanced into the living room, and kept walking. I watched her carefully, waiting for the painting to register. It didn't take long for her to do a comical double-take at the kitchen door. I laughed as she spun around, clapping her hands with glee. She ran over to the fireplace and gasped at the painting in wonder.

I came up from behind her and murmured into her ear, "Like it?"

"Yes, I love it! How did you manage to sneak that in?"

"I have my ways. I know how much you love this piece."

As the years went by, Paige and I kept our heads down and worked hard. I hadn't showered her with gifts like I'd wanted to, like I should have, even when we had the money. Paige would say that she isn't a materialistic person, and, although that's true, she has an eye for quality and appreciates the finer things in life.

I needed to make up for lost time, and, so, when our wedding anniversary came around, I tricked Paige into taking me to the mall to pick up my new glasses. When we were there, I guided her to a jewelry store and let her know that she could have any ring she wanted.

The look she gave me was infused with love and joy. "Really?"

"You deserve something better than that old gold-nugget thing I gave you years ago."

"I do," she said with a laugh.

The store was having a sale on loose diamonds. She could match any band with any diamond and create her own design. We pored over the choices for hours and finally ended up with a legendary ring that everyone in the store would talk about for years to come.

As she held the ring in her hand, I spoke from my heart, telling her how much I loved her, thanking her for being there for me, through sickness and in health, for richer or poorer, and all the rest. I had really put those wedding vows to the test.

She embraced me, planting a passionate kiss on my lips in the middle of the store. It felt like I was playing a lead role in one of those romantic comedies, where the hero and heroine fight against all odds to survive life and be together. I could almost feel the camera spinning around the store behind me.

◆ ◆ ◆

About a year later, on a lovely fall morning, Paige and I pulled up to our newly acquired corner lot. It overlooked a lake where I could see fish jumping out of the water, just teasing me to throw my line in.

We were scheduled to meet our architect but were a bit early. As I looked out over the property, I pictured our dream home being built in stages. The lot was perfect and in such high demand that the moment we closed on it, we received an offer to sell for a profit. I declined. You can't put a price tag on your dreams.

"Can you believe we've come this far?" I whispered. "We did it."

Paige smiled. "I was just thinking the same thing. Despite your hard-fought battle, we have our health. On top of that, we have a successful business and two amazing girls we get to work with every day."

"Do you think they'll always want to work in the family business?"

"Hard to say, but for now, I couldn't be happier to hear their friendly voices when I call the office."

I nodded. "They're growing up."

She looked out over the land in front of us. "Fast-forward a few years, and they'll get married and might just have children of their own."

I shook my head. "They'll always be baby girls to me."

She leaned over to me, wrapping her arms around me. "Oh, come on. If you listen carefully, you can almost hear the squeals of our grandchildren coming from the pool."

I grinned. "And I'll be alive to play with them."

Epilogue

RODNEY

AS I PULLED INTO THE PARKING LOT of Dr. A.'s office, with Paige by my side, I braced myself for the depression that always hit me. I would probably recognize a few faces, but some of his patients wouldn't be there, and I didn't care to dwell on that.

I glanced over at my wife and saw that she was deep in thought, looking out the window. She was probably thinking the same thing.

"Are you ready to go in?" I asked.

"As ready as I'll ever be."

As we walked through the front door, hand in hand, it felt like we'd just stepped out of a time machine. I instantly flashed back to the first time we'd sat down in that waiting room, bewildered and confused, wondering what would happen next, terrified for my future.

Our world had changed so much since then, but the patients who were sitting there, waiting to see Dr. A., were still living a nightmare.

How many were just receiving the fateful news that day?

Once we checked in, we were quickly ushered into the back room for the routine blood draw. Once I had the symbolic red bandage on my arm, I was taken to a small examination room to wait. It didn't take long for the red-haired nurse to come in.

"How are you?" she asked with her signature cheerful smile.

"Good," I said. "How have you been?"

"I've been put on an annual checkup, just like you!"

I breathed a sigh of relief. She'd come out the other side of her personal bout with breast cancer. "That's great news! I'm happy for you."

"Thank you," she murmured as she took my blood pressure.

After taking the rest of my vitals, she picked up her clipboard and asked, "So, how many years has it been?"

"Eight."

"Wow, that's amazing! So, what are you currently taking?" Her eyes bore into me, and I knew she wanted to hear about my list of medications. I shook my head and laughed. "You know, I'm not taking any prescribed drugs."

Years ago, when she asked me this same question, I listed off all the supplements I'd been taking, hoping that she'd take some interest. After a minute or two, she stopped writing. "So you're not taking any real medication?"

"No."

Not on your life.

She gave a dismissive wave of her hand. "Well, we don't need to put all this stuff down."

After that visit, I'd stopped mentioning all the vitamins and enzymes. To this day, I don't think she believed I wasn't taking any prescription drugs. It would just violate everything she'd been taught to believe. I think it was just easier for her to believe I was lying.

It didn't take long for Dr. A. to come into the room. As always, we talked about my business and how things were going.

"I keep seeing your Stampsco trucks driving around town," he said.

I smiled. "Yes, business is booming."

After a few minutes, he did a cursory examination of my body, feeling all around, looking for tumors.

"You know, I tell my patients about you," he said.

"Really? What do you say?"

Could it be that he tells them about the protocol I've been on? Maybe after all these years of my remaining cancer free, he'd finally come around. Wouldn't it be great if some of these patients were given a chance to survive without going through the pain and suffering of chemotherapy and radiation?

He beamed at me. "I tell them that you've been on watch-and-wait for eight years and that you are a living example of spontaneous remission. It gives them hope!"

False hope . . . Man, I wish I could talk to them.

After he was done with the examination, he nodded at me. "You're one of the healthiest lymphoma patients I've ever seen!"

I thanked him, and we agreed to schedule our next appointment for one year's time. I kept these appointments because I wanted to keep a record of everything to do with my recovery. Besides, if something were to come back, Pamela could do something about it if we caught it early. However, to date, the cancer markers haven't made another appearance.

We said our goodbyes to Dr. A. Then Paige and I walked into the elevator. I noticed another man inside with a red bandage on his arm.

"I see that you're in the red-armband club, too!" I said.

He grinned. "Yeah, I am."

"How's everything going?"

"The doctors and nurses really care about their patients here. I especially like the red-haired nurse. She always has a smile for me."

Paige and I looked at each other. "Yeah, we like her, too," I said.

"Do you have cancer?" he asked me.

"Non-Hodgkin's lymphoma."

He shook his head. "I'm on my third battle with throat cancer."

"I'm sorry to hear that."

He looked me up and down. "You look great. Are you in remission?"

"No, I'm cancer free. It's been gone for eight years now."

He whistled low. "Wow! That's encouraging. What's your secret?"

I grinned at him and said, "Buy me a glass of vegetable juice, and I'll tell you the story."

Cancer Heroes

ENZYME TREATMENT TESTIMONIALS

Barry Reisig—Las Vegas, NV
10-Year Victory over Pancreatic Cancer

BARRY, A 68-YEAR-OLD BUSINESS OWNER, was riding his snow-mobile at his hunting and fishing lodge in Utah in 2008, when he experienced excruciating pain in his abdomen and back. After making his way back to the lodge and returning home, he went to a hospital back in Las Vegas. While he thought kidney stones might be the cause, once his doctor ran a few tests, he advised Barry that it might be something more serious, and referred him to the Mayo Clinic.

At the Mayo Clinic, they ran a gamut of tests including a biopsy, which confirmed he had pancreatic cancer. The doctors advised Barry to undergo a Whipple procedure, also known as a pancreaticoduodenectomy. It's a complex operation involving the removal of the head of the pancreas, the first part of the small intestine (duodenum), the gallbladder and the bile duct, and then followed by chemotherapy.

Barry called a friend, an internist, and asked for advice. His friend said there may be another option, as he'd heard that some were having success with a pancreatic enzyme treatment, and referred Barry to Pamela McDougle. Barry followed up with Pamela to discuss the enzyme protocol.

Barry felt that the enzyme treatment was his best option, so he started on the program immediately. For roughly three years, he took 72 enzyme pills a day, plus supplements. He drastically changed his diet, used a near-infrared sauna daily, and did two coffee enemas daily. Barry's now on a maintenance dose of the enzymes daily, still eats healthy and says he feels great. It's been 10 years since his diagnosis, and he is now 78 years young and cancer-free!

Eddie Lamarre—Boston, MA
8-Year Victory over B-Cell Lymphoma

In 2010, Ed, a 66-year-old mechanic and truck driver, noticed a lump on his neck and visited his doctor for evaluation. After having blood tests and diagnostics performed, the doctor recommended they remove the lump from his neck and have it biopsied. The pathology came back positive for B-Cell Lymphoma.

Lymphomas are blood cancers in the lymph nodes. Conventional treatment includes radiation and chemotherapy. The doctor urged Ed to start chemo and radiation immediately. The news of a cancer diagnosis can be overwhelming, and Ed wanted a few days to think about it. Ed and his wife talked about treatment options, and his wife contacted a nutritionist she knew. The nutritionist said that while she couldn't help with Ed's cancer, she knew someone who could. She referred them to a medical doctor, who then referred Pamela McDougle and the pancreatic enzyme program.

After Ed discussed the details of the enzyme treatment with Pamela, he decided against chemo and radiation, and opted to start the enzyme protocol immediately.

Ed followed the daily enzyme and supplement protocol, began the daily coffee enemas, and made the necessary changes to his diet as recommended on the program. Over the first few months, Ed lost about 30lbs while on the program. His weight eventually stabilized and he continued on the full enzyme protocol for 12 months.

Ed is now cancer-free, and it's been 8 years since his diagnosis. He continues on the recommended maintenance dosage of the enzymes, and continues to visit his oncologist for annual checkups. Ed says he's grateful that his five grandchildren and eight great-grandchildren still have a grandfather. He spends as much time as he can with them out on the lake boating, tubing and swimming.

Acknowledgments

THANK YOU, PAMELA MCDOUGLE, from the bottom of our hearts, for your tireless efforts in supporting cancer patients the world over. Thank you for helping us through one of the most difficult times in our lives. Your commitment to continuing Dr. Kelley's legacy, in the face of ridicule and institutional opposition, has saved countless lives. Your knowledge, caring and compassion are truly unparalleled.

To Jessika and Jade, the most beautiful daughters any parents could ever hope for. We're truly sorry you had to share our battle with cancer during your childhood, but we're so blessed by and thankful for all your love and help. Your hugs and kisses made our dark days bright. And Jessika, you were right; we definitely had "better days inside." We love you both more than you will ever know.

Dr. George Yu, we are deeply indebted to you for taking time out of your busy schedule to write such a wonderful foreword for our book. It's doctors like you who are making a real difference in the world of cancer treatment. yufoundation.org

Donald Guy, we're so grateful for your guidance, love and support. You were truly "a friend who sticks closer than a brother" during our time of distress." (Proverbs 18:24)

A big thank-you to my aunt Cecille Skaggs for helping us weave both of our books into one. Wow, what an undertaking! Assisting us with this seemingly impossible task was hugely generous, and we'll be forever grateful.

Bruce Fox, thank you for your love and support. You were truly a "hiding place from the wind, a place of concealment from the rainstorm" for our entire family. (Isaiah 32:2)

To all our employees at STAMPSCO, past and present, we can't begin to express how much we appreciate your tireless help in carrying the load of responsibility during our fight with cancer. Simply put, we couldn't have done it without you.

Thank you to all of our STAMPSCO customers, vendors and industry colleagues. Thank you for all your support during these trying times, and for your ongoing confidence in our company.

Thank you to Dr. A and our entire cancer-care team for your professionalism, kindness and compassion. While we know it's not easy dealing with epic stubbornness like ours, we sincerely appreciate your respecting our right to choose our own treatment course, and your willingness to support our decision.

Laura Sherman, thank you for helping us to get our words out of our heads and down on paper! You're awesome and your writing skills are second to none! https://laurasherman.com

A big thank-you to Peter Bowerman, our Well-Fed publishing coach! From our title and back cover to the final pages of our book, it's been a pleasure working with you over the years. You are a true professional and excellent at what you do. Even as we write this, you are helping us meet our publishing deadline! Anyone considering publishing a book should put your name at the top of their list. http://www.wellfedsp.com.

Thank you Michele DeFilippo, Ronda Rawlins, Amy Collins and the entire crew at 1106 Design! From cover design to layout and editing, your services are exceptional. Thank you for your professionalism and guidance. https://1106design.com

Thank you, Marshall Hawkins with Sundance Photography for making us look better than we actually do! It's no mystery why you're the top-rated photographer in OKC. http://sundancephotographyokc.com

Thank you, Adrienne Bashita for getting our CIP Data Block finished so quickly and doing a great job! http://cipblock.com

A very special thanks to Barry Reisig and Eddie Lamarre for your willingness to share your personal cancer stories with us, and allowing us to use your testimonials in our book.

About the Authors

Rodney Stamps is a cancer survivor, cancer researcher, author, and public speaker. He is the Chairman of the Fire Systems Design Group, a global Fire Alarm Design and Engineering firm, and is CEO of STAMPSCO Fire & Security, Inc. based in Oklahoma City, Oklahoma.

Rodney has 30 years in the Fire & Life Safety industry, holds a NICET Level IV certification in Fire Alarm systems, and is a member of both the National Fire Protection Association and the American Society of Certified Engineering Technicians. He has been featured in numerous media outlets including *Fox, NewsOK, The Outlook Magazine, Security Sales & Integration, Security Systems News, Security Dealer & Integrator*, and *Fire Protection Engineering* Magazine.

Paige Lenington-Stamps, an author and cancer researcher, left her stay-at-home-mom life—taking care of her two daughters, Jessika and Jade—and strapped on a tool belt as a technician to help her husband build their fledgling company. She is currently Executive VP of the Fire Systems Design Group, and the President of STAMPSCO Fire & Security.

Paige is NICET Level II certified in Fire Alarm systems and has been featured in numerous media outlets including *Fox, Security Sales & Integration, Security Dealer & Integrator,* and in *Security Systems News* piece entitled "Women Gain Visibility, Power in Industry."

Rodney and Paige are co-founders of AttackingCancer.org.

KEEP UP THE FIGHT WITH THESE "MUST-HAVE" *ATTACKING CANCER* RESOURCES!

The Cancer Answer: *The Proven Alternative Protocol with a 97% Success Rate!*

Just what it says: The specific "how-two" details of what we did to beat my cancer—at every phase of the process. If I did it, it's in this book!

Format: Softcover, E-Book (Instant Download) Grab your copy at **www.attackingcancer.org/canceranswer**

The *Heal*Thy Body Cookbook: *A Tasty Collection of Healing, Cancer Fighting Recipes (80+% of Recipes Protocol-Compliant). A Side Dish to The Cancer Answer.*

While fighting cancer means making significant changes in your diet, you'd be amazed at how tasty these healthy recipes are!

Format: Softcover, E-Book (Instant Download) Get your copy at **www.attackingcancer.org/healthybody**

ONE-ON-ONE COACHING

Looking for some more dedicated attention on the journey to kicking your cancer to the curb? Rodney and Paige are taking on a limited number of coaching clients.

For all the details, visit **www.attackingcancer.org/coachme**

Don't forget to regularly visit www.attackingcancer.org, where you'll find plenty of free resources, and opportunities to connect with folks like yourself!

CPSIA information can be obtained
at www.ICGtesting.com
Printed in the USA
FFHW021656130219
50546523-55832FF